TELLING LIES

STEVE THRIFT

First published in 2023 by:
Britain's Next Bestseller
An imprint of
Live It Ventures LTD
126 Kirkleatham Lane, Redcar.
Cleveland.
TS10 5DD

Copyright © 2023 by Steve Thrift

The moral right of Steve Thrift to be identified as the author of this work has been asserted by him in accordance with the Copyright, Designs and Patents Act 1988.

All rights reserved.

No part of this book may be reproduced or transmitted in any form or any means without written permission from the copyright holder. A catalogue record for this book is available from the British Library. All characters appearing in this work are fictitious. Any resemblance to real persons, living or dead, is purely coincidental.

@BNBSbooks

Cover design: Ashley Wood (Crafter Studio 24)

ISBN - 978-1-914907-21-0

Printed in the U.K

'Whoever kills an innocent person, it is as if he has killed all humanity'

QURAN 5:32

*This book is dedicated to the memory of
Monika Elizabeth Zumsteg Telling
24th November 1956 – 29th March 1973*

For those who loved her and will always do so

INTRODUCTION

I have had no co-operation from the relevant authorities in writing this book at all, and little co-operation from individuals.

I first met the man who was named Michael Henry Maxwell Telling born, on his birth certificate in 1950, in January 1982.

The newspapers thought he was mad. I sincerely doubt it. What I have no doubt about is that he was a compulsive liar, and that he was a manipulative murderer and a coward.

I was a police officer, newly promoted to the dizzy heights of temporary detective. The meeting was because I was, as duty CID officer, had been called upon to arrest him for criminal damage that he had caused in a fit of rage. I was an authorised firearms officer, but my request to carry a firearm was denied, even though he was thought to have a gun in his home. When I went to his home address, things were not as expected. I arrested him, but for far more than criminal damage. When the matter was eventually heard at the Crown Court in Aylesbury, the hearing was 'In-camera'. No press or public were permitted to attend. In-camera is the opposite of trial in open court where all parties and witnesses testify in a public courtroom, and attorneys publicly present their arguments to the trier of fact.

Entire cases may be heard in-camera when, for example, matters of national security are involved. In-camera review by a judge may be used during otherwise open trials—for example, to protect trade secrets. It is unusual for a case such as this to be heard in such a way. National security and trade secrets were not involved.

What, and whom was involved was far more than that. The defendant was the heir to a vast multi-billion-pound fortune. His grandfather was, and at the time of writing still is the richest man in the United Kingdom. Money talks, the guilty walk.

The trial did nothing to curtail his lust for the unusual. His fortune, his marriage to a Californian beauty were not enough. His vast collection of fast cars and motorcycles, and access to money was not enough. Nothing was ever enough for Michael Telling.

The result of the Aylesbury trial shaped his entire future. A small fine meant nothing to him. He had got away with it. The fantasist had won.

The result led to murder and a life of fantasy. The sensational details, and the lies told in court worked. The story reads like fiction but it is fact.

My attempt to write this story has taken many

years. There has been no co-operation whatsoever from the Thames Valley Police, The Devon and Cornwall Police, the relevant Police Commissioners, the Home Office or the Australian Federal Police, and numerous others named at the end of this book.

All attempts to contact Lord Vestey have remained unanswered. All others are noted at the end of this book. The conspiracy of silence has lasted for nearly 40 years.

It is abundantly clear that Telling was, and remains, an embarrassment to the Vestey family, and rightly so.

This story has never been correctly told before by someone who met and spent time with both Telling and his wife Monika.

Her sister Riki, and her friend Christina have been amazing in their support and contributions.

The story of the real-life Billy Liar can finally be told. The story of Michael Henry Maxwell Telling. A liar, fantasist, coward and a murderer. The lie that he lived until his dying day.

Riki and Christina – thank you.

I thank you both for your time and memories.

I write this book out of respect for Monika.

STEVEN THRIFT

CHAPTER
ONE

And yet, strange to say, now that the truth is recognized by most cultivated people...now more than ever, in the history of the world, are they doing all they can to further the survival of the unfittest. — **Herbert Spencer**

LET me make this very clear from the outset.

I did not like Michael Telling,

I had no respect for him whatsoever. He has variously been described as a handsome young man. I found him to be an insignificant little man, who needed to prove something to the world. He had a beautiful young wife who he constantly berated and frightened. Michael Telling was a bully. A bully only to women. He terrorised and murdered. He was deluded and illiterate. Who needs education when you are the heir to a multimillion-pound fortune.? Why would you need to work a day in your life? He did not. He had all the trappings that money could buy. He had many expensive motor vehicles and several dozen exclusive motorbikes, including two California Highway Patrol Harley Davidson's, and to complete the picture, the full C.H.I.P.S uniform. My belief is that he saw himself as Erik Estrada playing Officer Francis 'Ponch' Poncherello from the popular TV series of the day. He had everything a life of excess could possibly buy. But I am getting ahead of myself. More of that later.

I got to know Michael Telling in the months after I had arrested him, and after he had booked himself into the finest mental institutes that his inherited money could buy. He was feigning mental illness to avoid trial and imprisonment. It was one of what was to be many meetings at similar institutions in the United Kingdom over a period of time.

One of the things that he told with me, stuck with me. I clearly remember what he said to me.

"I didn't have the best start in life. I was born in New York at the Mortimer B. Zuckerman Hospital on the 25th floor. My father came to see me. My mother told me he said nothing, just jumped out of the hospital window to his death." Poor man. What a horrible start in life. I felt compassion for the man. He appeared upset, even all these years later. He was., after all, talking about his father.

It was a complete lie. Michael Telling was born in Tunbridge Wells, England. His father was Henry Willis Maxwell Telling. He died at the age of 74 on 4th August 1993 of natural causes. He was still alive when he was talking about his father's suicide.

This was the start of very many lies, that the real life Walter Mitty made up to make people either feel sorry for him, or to be in awe of him. The American Heritage Dictionary defines a Walter Mitty as an ordinary often ineffectual person who indulges in fantastic daydreams of personal triumphs.

The definition of evil should be: - the quality of being morally bad or something that causes harm or misfortune. An example of an evil is discrimination. A better example is Michael Henry Maxwell Telling.

The feeling sorry for him bit nearly worked for me. Thankfully though, only nearly.

Michael Telling was a truly evil man and a coward. His actions proved that point beyond a shadow of a doubt, as you will see.

CHAPTER TWO

JOYCE VESTEY WAS BORN on 2ⁿᵈ September 1920.

She was the eldest child of Hilda Dorothy Thompson and Hon. Leonard Vestey, Lord Vestey and she was born into a life of plenty.

Her father, William Vestey, was born on 21 January 1859. He came from an old Liverpool family of traders. In 1876, at the age of seventeen, he was sent to Chicago by his father Samuel Vestey, a provisioner of Liverpool.

He first managed a meat canning factory that was financed by his father. Together with his younger brother Edmund, he established Vestey Brothers (which later became the Vestey Group) in 1897 from a family butchery business in Liverpool. They were pioneers of refrigeration, opening a cold store in London in 1895.

The Vestey brothers then went to South America in an attempt to make a fortune because the economy there was booming. They started by buying game birds and storing them in the cold stores of American companies before shipping them to Liverpool. These early activities soon developed into importing beef and beef products into the UK, which in turn led to them owning cattle ranches in Brazil, Venezuela and Australia, and their own meat processing factories in Argentina, Uruguay, New Zealand and Australia. In 1914, they built a meat processing works at Bullocky Point, Darwin, Australia, but closed its operations in 1920 after the Darwin Rebellion.

They acquired the 3,000-square-kilometre, 1,200 square miles, Wave Hill Station in the Northern Territory of Australia, in 1914. At that time, legislation permitted Aboriginal Australian workers to be paid in tea, tobacco and other rations. The Vestey's refused to pay their workers in wages, leading to tensions and arguments from the beginning, which continued until the Wave Hill walk-off, a strike that lasted for eight years.

Little is known about her mother, Hilda Dorothy Thompson except to say that she was born in Grays, Essex, England on 30 March 1890 to Thomas Thompson and Caroline Brunker. Hilda Dorothy Thompson married Leonard Vestey and had 2 children, Joyce and her sister Elizabeth. She divorced Vestey in 1931, and passed away on 21 Jun 1943 in Chelmsford, Essex, England.

During World War I another Vestey company, the Blue Star Line , was a major supplier of Argentine beef to England, and it was for this service to the wartime provisioning of England that William Vestey was later raised to the peerage. He was made a Baronet of Bessemer House in the Metropolitan Borough of Camberwell on 21 June 1913, and Baron Vestey, of Kingswood in the County of Surrey on 20 June 1922.

This was a surprise because back in 1915, the brothers, after being refused a request for income tax exemption made to David Lloyd George, moved to Buenos Aires to avoid paying income tax in the UK. They objected to paying income tax, as similar US companies could sell their wares in the United Kingdom and also at home in the USA without the necessity of actually paying tax on their profits. So then, why should they be treated differently? Why should they pay any income tax. They were, after all, providing a service to the United Kingdom. The family later administered the business through a Paris trust that enabled it to legally avoid UK tax until the loophole was closed in 1991. From 1915 to 1918, they moved to Chicago then to Argentina and back to England.

During that time, William Vestey commented, very publicly on his tax position, 'The current position suits me admirably. I am abroad, I pay nothing'. He cocked a very public snook at the United Kingdom. Cocking a snook is a sign of derision or contempt, made by putting the thumb on the nose, holding the palm open and perpendicular to the face, and wiggling the remaining fingers. It is used mostly by schoolchildren, often combined with verbal insults, sticking out the tongue or blowing a raspberry.

He certainly showed contempt, and when one peer

in the House Of Lords demanded sometime later that William explain his actions, William refused to do so.

At that time, Prime Minister Lloyd George was offering knighthoods throughout the British Empire for the genuinely princely sum of £20,000. The inflation rate at that time was 15%, and at today's values, £20,000 now equates to just under one million pounds. A small price some may say, and some indeed did say. Previously unheard of, because of their attitude and desertion during wartime to South America, members of Parliament publicly denounced the Vesteys, and the honour bestowed on the now Baron William Vestey, as reported in the honours list in 1922.

King George V sent a letter to Lloyd George on 3rd July 1922. It is now a matter of public record and is currently in the House Of Lords Records Office:-

'My Dear Prime Minister,

I cannot conceal from you my profound concern at the very disagreeable situation that has arisen on the question of honours. The peerage that I was advised to confer upon Sir William Vestey have brought things rather to a climax; though for some time there have been evident signs of growing public dissatisfaction on account of the excessive number of honours being conferred, the personality of some of the recipients, and the questionable circumstances in which some of the honours have been granted. In recent years there have been instances in which honours have been bestowed where subsequent information has betrayed a lack of care in the enquires made as to the fitness of the person selected for recognition. I do appeal most strongly for the establishment of some efficient and trustworthy procedure in order to protect The Crown and the government from the possibility of similar, if not humiliating incidents, the recurrence of which must inevitably constitute an evil, dangerous to the social and political well being of the state.'

Lloyd George attempted to defend his methods, but stated that he was unaware of Vestey's tax avoidance and apparent wartime desertion to South America, and that if he had been aware he would not have put him forward for a barony.

But in any event it was all too little, too late. Despite the royal outcry and the Prime Minister's regret, the dropout child from Liverpool became Baron Vestey of Kingswood, Surrey.

The purchased gold coronet followed as did the commissioned family crest and motto of *E Labore Stabilitas* – From Labour, Stability. Unfortunately that stability would not follow the patrilineality, also known as the male line, the spear side or agnatic kinship, certainly not in the case of Michael Telling.

Henry Willis Maxwell Telling was born on 6 February 1919 at Lewisham, Kent, England. He was the son of Harry George Telling and Edith Willis. He married Joyce Vestey, daughter of Hon. Leonard Vestey and Hilda Dorothy Thompson, on 16 February 1949.1 He and Joyce Vestey were divorced in 1953.

Michael Henry Maxwell Telling was their only child. Telling's second cousin, Lord Vestey, at that time had a fortune estimated at $900 million based on 250

Vestey companies in 27 countries that make the Vestey's the world's largest meat retailers. They are best known as the founders and owners of the Fray Bentos food brand.

The Fray Bentos food brand is associated with tinned processed meat products, originally corned beef and, latterly, meat pies. The brand has been sold in the United Kingdom, other European countries, and Australia. Created in the latter half of the 19th century, the name is derived from the port of Fray Bentos in Uruguay where the products were originally processed and packaged.

In 1924, Liebig Extract of Meat Company, together with the Fray Bentos brand, was acquired by then what was known as the Vestey Group who renamed the Uruguayan operation Frigorífico Anglo del Uruguay, also known as the Anglo Meatpacking Company.

Fray Bentos's heyday was in World War II. The family business sold an estimated seventy percent of all meat consumed in Great Britain. The businesses extended to France, Spain, Portugal, United States of America, Venezuela, Argentina, Paraguay, South Africa, Australia, New Zealand, Madagascar and Brazil, and vast areas of land in each country. As a supplier of meat to the Allies, Fray Bentos shipped more than 16 million cans of corned beef to Europe in 1943 alone. British soldiers serving in North Africa during the desert campaign called it Desert Chicken. The Anglo factory in Fray Bentos, at its height, employed over 5,000 workers from more than 50 countries to process 400 cows an hour. As a result of the demand for Fray Bentos products at this time the Uruguayan currency for the only time in history became more valuable than the US dollar.

Just before the German occupation of France, the trusts and fortune were moved to Paraguay, a neutral country - and the business continued to grow, and all profits remained tax free.

Baron Vestey died in 1940, but assured his heirs future by issuing a directive that they should surely 'extend good offices and extend pecuniary and other assistance to those other members of the family according to their merits and needs. Family members in England continued to receive discretionary payments from the trust, again tax free.

In 1948, the Inland Revenue of Great Britain, a department of the government, complained to the Law Lords that the Vestey's were evading income tax by forming foreign trusts and avoiding tax anywhere in the world, surely due from its vast international empire. The Lords accepted the position of the Inland Revenue, and directed that all income, wherever derived from should be subject of British tax. They then interpreted the victory as the ability to tax all heirs to William and Edmund's fortunes. However, Inland Revenue backed down somewhat, and agreed to only tax some portion of the fortune at some stage in the future. This legal argument continued for the next sixty years, ending in 1979 with The Vestey's winning.

Oddly the Courts overturned the previous ruling, and stated that tax should only be imposed on the creators of foreign trusts and not any living descendants. It also found that the Inland Revenue had been unconstitutional because in the United Kingdom Parliament alone had the authority to fix taxes, not the administrative agency of the government called Inland Revenue.

This meant that legally, all descendants, including Michael Telling, could continue to receive income from the trusts completely tax free in the United Kingdom.

In the immediate post-war years, the Fray Bentos products were a staple food in Britain. The product range was expanded to include canned meat pies such as steak and kidney and minced beef and onion. In 1958, Vestey began manufacturing Fray Bentos pies in England, and production was moved to a plant in the London Borough of Hackney. In 1964, the use of the brand for corned beef was significantly damaged when an outbreak of typhoid in Aberdeen, in which three people died, was traced to a tin of Fray Bentos corned beef imported from South America. The corned beef had been contaminated as a result of the cooling process during manufacture, in which the untreated water used had come from a river into which an estimated 66 tonnes of human excrement and 250,000 gallons of urine entered every day.

At the end of the 1960's, Vestey disposed of the Anglo factory to the Uruguayan government and, in 1968, sold Liebig to Brooke Bond, for an undisclosed amount, but very many millions of dollars.

Monika Elizabeth Zumsteg was born on 24th November 1956 in Oakland, Alameda County, California, USA. Monika was the daughter of Santa Rosa business consultant Louis Zumsteg and his wife, Elsa.

A naturally beauty, she became a beauty queen and a popular member of her college and society. She was intelligent, and destined for great things, until she was introduced to Michael Telling by her father, Leo Zumsteg, a motorcycle aficionado.

It was the worst mistake of his life, and one that he regretted until his dying day.

CHAPTER
THREE

Truth is stranger than fiction, but it is because fiction is obliged to stick to possibilities: truth isn't.' – **Mark Twain**

Tis strange – but true, for truth is always strange, stranger than fiction. – **Lord Byron**

"I DIDN'T HAVE the best start in life. I was born in New York," he lied.

It was fiction, one of many lies that he told throughout his entire life, and one of many that he told me. On reflection, I believe that he actually believed some of his outrageous lies, as he became embroiled in them to such an extent that extraction was impossible. I do not know if Michael Telling actually knew what was truth and what was fiction, I do not think he could tell the difference. He had indeed had the very best start in life, and was heir to a multi-million-pound fortune. The trouble was that he did not make the best of his fortunate position and his inherited fortune.

Fortune led to complacency.
Complacency led to recklessness.
Recklessness led to stupidity.
Stupidity led to a very grisly murder.

CHAPTER FOUR

'Remember, it's your ATTITUDE, not your APTITUDE, that determines your ALTITUDE!' – **Zig Ziglar**

TO BE successful in any area in life you need to have the right attitude, which means you have to approach any task or job with determination, tenacity and above all plenty of enthusiasm.

Michael Henry Maxwell Telling was born on 17th May 1950. His parents were Henry Willis Maxwell Telling and Joyce Vestey. The 28 year-old Joyce was the daughter of Leonard Vestey. Leonard Vestey was born on 21 December 1888.1 He was the third son of William Vestey, 1st Baron Vestey and Sarah Ellis. He married, firstly, Hilda Dorothy Thompson, daughter of Thomas Thompson, on 21 August 1919, having returned to the country after World War 1 where he gained the rank of Captain in the Royal Field Artillery. He was called a rouge, cad and a bounder at the time, having abandoned his wife and six year old daughter for his mistress in 1926. He and Hilda Dorothy Thompson were divorced in 1931.

Young Joyce grew up in a world of untold riches, and was nurtured and protected by a procession of governesses and nannies, and knew little love. She in turn found it difficult to give love to Henry, or the young Michael. Money can't buy you love or happiness apparently.

Michael's father, Henry, was a violent drunk, as Joyce found out to her cost. The pregnancy proved problematic, and as a baby, Michael was a feeble child, born at 5 ½ pounds weight, and prone to every childhood illness going as an infant. He lived with his parents in a London mansion, but in a separate wing, and he, like his mother, was nurtured by a succession of governesses and nannies, and rarely saw or had any contact with his parents. He certainly did not receive their love. As an adult he could remember hearing them shouting at each other through the walls in their many arguments. The young Michael was completely starved of affection, save the little that he could ring out of his nursing staff, who were dismissed with unusual regularity.

On reflection, Joyce was clearly distancing herself from the child, exactly as she had been from a young age. She found him hard, if not impossible to love or even show genuine affection for. She neither knew nor gave affection or love to her child. He disliked contact with others and was a fidgety child, prone to tantrums, especially if a pleasant and affectionate nanny had been recently dismissed.

Henry and Joyce were divorced on 21 May 1953, and Michael was 3 years old. As part of the divorce, the boy was awarded to his mother but there was no love shown, and they did not share a single meal. He was pandered to by another succession of paid help in the form of nannies, nursemaids and au-pairs. This staff were told to keep the child away from home for as long as possible each day.

He was five years old before he was diagnosed with diabetes, and at that age, in order that she see even less of the boy, he was sent to North Bridge House school in St. John's Wood, London. St John's Wood is a district in the City of Westminster, west London. It is an affluent neighbourhood, and the fifth most expensive in London. St John's Wood tenants pay the highest average rent in London, and private schools are expensive. But particularly with inherited money, nothing is too much for one's children. Nothing that is, except for love.

The strange child that was Michael Telling remained at the private institution for 18 months, until at 6 1/2 years old he was expelled for throwing lighted matches at his classmates. Even at the tender age of 6 1/2, the young Michael was spiralling out of control.

Shortly afterwards, Joyce moved to Dulwich an area of south London, an even more desirable area, favoured by many actors and politicians. In the closing chapter of Charles Dickens' romance The Pickwick Papers, Samuel Pickwick retires to a house in Dulwich, described as - 'one of the most pleasant spots near London.'

The move did not affect the young Michael, as

shortly afterwards, he was accepted at a boarding school. Pinehurst school in St. Catherine's, Kent was a long-sought solution for such parents and students struggling in the public-school system: a private boarding school tailored to students with learning disabilities and behavioural issues. So, ideal for young Michael. It was a small Victorian house with few inmates, maybe twenty or so in total.

But it did not go well. Shortly after arriving there, the 7, year old broke into the school tuck shop and stole sugar related products such as sweets and cake, and suffered a self-induced diabetic coma, but whilst conscious he demanded to be returned home. It failed and he stayed.

But once again, he broke into the tuck shop. This time as the sugary treats had failed, he stole money for the public transport fare home. When he arrived there, he lied to his mother that the school had been destroyed by fire. Having discovered that the story was fiction, Joyce told the child that he had to return to the school. He threw another tantrum and took off his clothes and threw himself down into the road and into the path of motor cars. He did, however, run out of the way before he was hit by any, and he was returned to the school.

He played truant on many more occasions, turning up unannounced at relative's homes, throwing himself upon their mercy. All pleas went unheard, and the ruse failed. He returned to the school.

He was still a sickly child, needing twice daily insulin injections. Still small for his age, slight, underweight and short for his age, liable to catch any childhood illness that was going, and frankly a total disaster at any sports, he was vulnerable and unpopular. In addition to his unpopularity with the others, he totally hated being there. The smallest, most feeble child there was also by far the richest, and as he continued throughout his life, he purchased friendship, and was victim to several older and bigger predators.

The headmistress at the time, a spinster by the name of Feek, considered the child to be a fake, a malingerer. Malingering is the fabrication, feigning, or exaggeration of physical or psychological symptoms designed to achieve a desired outcome, in this case, pity. She further considered him to be a manipulative liar – all at the ripe old age of seven. He remained this way for the whole of his life.

He was relentlessly bullied, and by this time he was already a heavy smoker. He stole money from his mother as the membership fee to be in gangs, but he was still not allowed in. By this time, after brief visits home on holidays, on being told that he must return to Pinehurst, he would fly into a now violent rage, kicking out at his mother, and smashing toys. He seemed to learn absolutely nothing at the school, except the ability to swear, but at least the troublesome child was away from home, and at least then he was the responsibility of someone other than his mother.

After two years, having gained no education and failing miserably to persuade the doting mother to remove him from the school, things took another turn. In the dark of night, he crept downstairs to a storage area beneath the stairs. There was a pile of mattresses stored there and Michael set fire to them. At nine years old he was drinking sherry and smoking heavily. He kept carving knives in his room.

The smoke awoke Miss Feek, who extinguished the blaze before much damage was caused. Michael got his wish though, and he was duly expelled from that school. Expelled from two expensive private schools by the age of 10.

Little changed. The violent spats continued, and soon he was out of control. After several incidents he removed knives from the kitchen, and when asked for them he threatened to kill Joyce with them.

Visits to physiatrists and psychologists followed, and at ten years and two weeks of age, Michael Telling was admitted to Maudsley Hospital in London, the most expensive and exclusive psychiatric private institution that money could buy. He again hated the place. He failed to communicate with other patients, and formed a deep mistrust of them – thinking that they were after his money. Two and a half years of tests and more tests followed. His IQ was tested. An Intelligence Quotient indicates a person's mental abilities relative to others. Everyone has numerous specific mental abilities, some of which can be measured accurately and are reliable predictors of academic and financial success.

On most intelligence tests, average IQ score is 100. Michael Telling scored 110, but he was found to have little self-esteem, but conversely the best care that money could buy found him egocentric and had little reading, writing or mathematical skills.

Hospital records note that had violent behaviour,

and fits of temper led to him destroying items when he could not get his own way. He was almost a kleptomaniac, constantly stealing worthless items. He failed to submit or to adhere to any form of authority or discipline. A petulant child with little interest in others.

And yet he was released and was returned for a second time to Pinehurst.

CHAPTER
FIVE

He who opens a school door, closes a prison. -
Victor Hugo

LIFE AT PINEHURST school continued much as it had done before Michael's enforced absence.

He continued to be disruptive, but his private medical staff decided that he was cured of his maladies, and should be transferred to a 'normal' school.

Although 'normal', the unfortunate institution was The William Penn comprehensive school in Red Post Hill, Post Hill, North Dulwich. Over the years the school gained a bad reputation and in later years it was renamed 'Dulwich High School for Boys', but it was just as bad (maybe worse - the pupils tried to burn it down) and was eventually closed. Richard Feakin was a teacher there. He said, "I was a student teacher at William Penn in 1963 and have little recall of any of the students' names. However, I do remember

Telling probably because of the Freddie and the Dreamers hit I'm Telling You Now. He was a little immature boy who I am sure had a difficult time at such a macho establishment".

It is surely coincidence that Kingsdale School just up the road from William Penn was built on the former Vestey Estate in the 1950s. At the end of World War II Lord Vestey proposed turning Kingswood into a hostel for his employees but London's housing needs were so great that in 1946 the London County Council announced a compulsory purchase order for Kingswood. It acquired a total of 37 acres of which 30 acres was set aside for housing development and about three and a half acres allocated for the school. Kingsdale House is still there and used by the school as an off-site centre.

Michael telling was a day pupil, and oddly continued to sleep at Maudsley hospital. This was unusual, but his mother made it abundantly clear that she was unable and unwilling to accept his disruptive, strange and violent behaviour, and did not want him at her home, even during school holidays. It seems that by this stage, her maternal love, which was previously lacking, had completely escaped her. During school recesses the unfortunate child was packed off to a state boarding school, care of London County Council. Post Hill, North Dulwich. London County Council (LCC) was the principal local government body for the County of London throughout its existence from 1889 to 1965, and later became known as the Greater London Council. The LCC inherited the powers, but had wider authority over matters such as education for the majority.

At the age of thirteen he was moved to another school, Bredinghurst, in Stuart Road, Peckham Rye, south east London. Like Pinehurst before it, it was a school for problem boys. It is a boys' secondary special school for students with odd behaviour, social and emotional difficulties. All students had special educational needs.

Many had additional special educational needs, in particular attention deficit hyperactivity disorder and speech, language and communication difficulties. The proportion of pupils known to need additional help was high compared to the national average.

This school no longer exists, and at the time of writing there is a major historical investigation under way into personal injury, loss and damage occasioned to former pupils as a result of alleged abuse and maltreatment suffered whilst they were pupils at the school.

The former pupils allege incidents of sexual, physical and emotional abuse whilst resident at Bredinghurst by members of staff and/or other residents. The alleged abuse of pupils, who were at their most vulnerable when they attended Bredinghurst, was obviously a gross breach of trust by the staff employed to care for and protect them. Instead of being a caring and nurturing environment, the former residents state that the school was an institute feared for its alleged brutal and abusive regimes. The abuse and maltreatment that the victims say they were subjected to whilst they were pupils at Bredinghurst has been varied in nature. The impact of that abuse upon their lives has been long-standing and serious. There is no evidence that Michael Telling was subject to any abuse there, one can only speculate. And if one speculates, what could the impact been on this vulnerable child?

What is known, is that he remained at the school for five years. He found it difficult to adjust and to interact with others. He was conscious of his then debilitating diabetes.

As a member of the British upper-class, the aristocracy, he would have, in normal circumstances, been expected to attend Oxbridge, either Oxford or Cambridge Universities, the premier learning institutions in the country, followed by officer entry as a graduate into the armed forces of the United Kingdom.

His status would have normally assured this to have happened. However, he was unable to pass the required examinations, let alone score highly enough for a place at Oxbridge.

In addition to this new defeat, his mother Joyce, remarried a man named Thomas Strong, and they both moved to South Africa.

Michael very much hoped to gain fruitful employment with one of the many Vestey companies, but he was neither wanted nor suitable, and in any event such practices were discouraged. The practice among those with power or influence of favouring relatives or friends, especially by giving them jobs.

And so, the young man lived in a central London hostel, paid for by generous annuities from his distant mother. Even though his residence lacked style, the money that he was given ensured that he had many boy's toys. A constant stream of gadgets and new motor cars followed. The life of excess had very much begun.

Unknown to Michael at the time, he would never work for the giant Vestey organisation. William and Edmond had established a strict line of succession in the business world, while providing for the rest of the family with untold riches at the age of 21.

Michael had a couple of years to go, and he managed to attain a job at a menswear shop. After six months, his sticky fingers assured that he was sacked for theft.

By this time, his mother and stepfather had moved to Australia, and Michael joined them there, and arrived in Sydney shortly before his 20th birthday. He found menial work on an assembly line, attained Australian citizenship and met a girl. She was pregnant when they met, through a rape. He was certain that they would marry, but she dumped him after the child was born.

He took an overdose, followed by a second overdose after being dumped by a second girlfriend. In each case it was an attention seeking effort. It did not work.

It seemed that for the next few years he was fairly stable, until he lost his job due to significantly cut or scale-back costs. This was due to excessively-high costs and low profitability (and unsustainable losses). And so, Michael was without work, but not without money. He decided that he would never work again, no need to do so after all, and he devoted his time to his toys, his guns, motorcycles and cars. He was an enthusiast of the then popular citizens band radio, and his reading consisted of magazines about mercenaries and special forces.

At this time, he met another girl, another love of his life, Alison Webber, a waitress who had been born in England. And the lies started, with gusto.

He told her that he had been an SAS soldier in Vietnam. After a year they married, and shortly afterwards Alison became pregnant. Because of this they both returned to England, to Devon. The Vestey trust purchased a house for them in Torquay, and their son Matthew was born there.

And so, the problems with the fantasist continued. Within a couple of years, Michael Telling was becoming bored, had a need for excitement in his life, and so he flew out to America, to California.

CHAPTER
SIX

> "The idea of 'California Girls' is that there's this guy who thinks about girls all the time, so much that he starts to imagine all kinds." - **Brian Wilson**

THE REASON for the trip to California was simple. Michael Telling, unemployed, and unemployable, needed to spend, to buy another motorcycle, specifically another Harley Davidson.

Everything to excess seemed to have been his motto in life from then on. After all, one can never have enough things, can one? Maybe more than one Harley. Why not? Money was no object. Having a wife and child in England made no difference to his wanderlust or love for spending.

From San Francisco he travelled the 2000 miles to Milwaukee, to the Harley Davidson factory. He wanted a VIP tour of the facility, and to put in his orders. He did both of these things. There would be many more visits and many more orders. The factory could not supply his wishes there and then, and so Michael returned to San Francisco, and immediately to the local dealer, Dudley Perkins in Mission Street, where they had a suitable machine in stock. He paid as usual by credit card. The cost was $7500, paid for on American Express.

The Harley-Davidson teams' mascot was a small pig, which they would take around the track with them on victory laps. Lawrence Weishaar was a Class A Racing Champion in the 1910's and 1920s. He rode for the Harley-Davidson 'Wrecking Crew,' and helped to popularize the nickname 'hog' in reference to Harley-Davidson by carrying the team's mascot, a small pig, around on victory laps. Weishaar was particularly fond of the brand, and many photographs exist of him and the pig. It is because of this mascot that Harley-Davidson motorcycles are called 'hogs.'

Harleys were very Marmite bikes – love them or hate them. On one side, supporters possess an incredibly loyal passion for the bike, while on the other side of the spectrum lies a severe distaste for the brand. There seem to be no in-betweens.

Like any other brand, Harley has had its fair share of issues. If you're a Harley-hater, you'll nod in agreement with the issues with these bikes. The brand has such a strong following that despite and in spite of all of these glaringly obvious and widely acknowledged issues, Harley Davidson maintains an enormous, dedicated, brand-loyal following. Their fan club spans across the globe and they aren't just providing lip service in their revere for these bikes, they're also dropping some big bucks to own, collect, and customize them – even though it's known that these pesky and costly issues exist. Never an issue though, with a never-ending supply of inherited money.

Some of the most glaring problems with Harley Davidson bikes that everyone who loves them chooses to ignore are;

So Many Recalls.

Expensive to Purchase.

Expensive to Insure.

They require constant upkeep.

Associated with bad boy, Hells Angel/Easy Rider Image

Poor handling

Conversely;

The sound of a Harley-Davidson engine is distinctive and

They look beautiful.

Over 100 motorcycle manufacturers in the USA no longer exists, Harley is the only one.

But even the greatest fans of the expensive and highly chromed machines have to admit to the inferiorities over some other motorcycles from overseas. The clutches were always stiff and difficult, the gearbox was very noisy, and the acceleration questionable at times. But they still looked beautiful.

All this good luck takes time to build. Triumph and Indian may claim longer histories but, with the possible exception of Royal Enfield, no motorcycle company has been in constant production longer than Harley-Davidson.

Lou Zumsteg understood the attraction, but he

preferred Japanese motor-cycles. He found them to be faster and agile than a cat burglar on cocaine. Lou owned eight such machines in 1980, as he rode through Sonoma Valley, to Sausalito in the shadow of the Golden Gate bridge in California.

Sausalito is in Marin County and is one of the best places to live in California. Living in Sausalito offers residents a dense suburban feel and most residents own their homes. The weather is wonderful, and on this Autumn day in 1980 the weather was unseasonably warm and sunny. Residents and visitors took advantage and many took the opportunity to eat crab, whilst admiring the view over San Francisco. The world-renowned bridge is named for the Golden Gate Strait, the narrow, turbulent, 300-foot-deep stretch of water below the bridge that links the Pacific Ocean on the west to San Francisco Bay on the east. As for the strait, its name slightly predates the 1849 start of the Gold Rush and was inspired by something else entirely. In 1846, when soldier, explorer and future presidential candidate John C. Fremont saw the watery trench that breached the range of coastal hills on the western edge of otherwise landlocked San Francisco Bay, it reminded him of another beautiful landlocked harbour, The Golden Horn of the Bosporus in Constantinople, now Istanbul. He named this part of California, 'The golden gate to the Orient'. A few hundred yards north of the red Golden Gate bridge, in Sausalito there are a lot of restaurants, coffee shops, and parks, with plunging hills and forests. Many retirees live in Sausalito and residents tend to be liberal in thought and deed.

Lou Zumsteg and his wife Elsa, rode the Yamaha that he had named Genghis from their home in Santa Rosa, around a fifty -mile trip on a beautiful Indian summer's day.

'It is absurd to divide people into good or bad. People are either charming or tedious', said Oscar Wilde.

I have to disagree with the above in this case. I found Michael Telling neither charming nor tedious, and he certainly was bad. He was now in the land of the free and the home of the brave, but he was neither free nor brave.

And so, he rode his new shiny Harley, with every possible extra added to it, in his Harley Davidson clothes and Harley Davidson cowboy boots, around the mid-west of America, and was soon to meet a man who would change his life, and the result would alter the life of many others. That man was business consultant Louis Zumsteg from Santa Rosa, California, another motorcycle enthusiast. His wife Elsa rode pillion on Lou's bike.

Louis had a young daughter named Monika. Louis would introduce Michael Telling to Monika. ~~It would be a decision that would haunt him until his dying day.~~

Lou Zumsteg made comment on the Harley - Davidson. Telling nodded acquiescence and asked Lou where he could park his bike. He said he wanted to see the town of Sausalito, and followed Lou to a parking lot a little way away.

The Englishman introduced himself, stated that had only been in the country for a short while, and that he had come over to buy this very motor cycle, the limited edition FXB Sturgis in black .

FSB Sturgis

Lou liked the machine, and Elsa liked the smooth-talking British stranger. Dressed in blue jeans, T shirt and leathers, for some reason, Lou found him good looking, and liked his nice smile.

She thought him a little shy and softly spoken, but put that down to being British and as such naturally reserved, but she had already decided that he came from good stock, proper breeding.

He would make the perfect partner for Monika, thought Elsa. Monika was young, free and single. She was also exceptionally intelligent and exceptionally beautiful, a great catch for any good- looking Englishman. In particular and Englishman who rode a motor cycle. The cogs were whirling, Elsa was already making plans in her head. She found him extremely deferential, respectful, civil and very polite. I would call it obsequious servile, ingratiating, unctuous and sycophantic.

The unsuspecting couple asked Telling to accompany them on their visit to the town, and he agreed. The couple and the English stranger got along well, and they enjoyed lunch together in a waterfront restaurant.

A throwaway comment led to the most negative change in the couple's lives. They invited him to Santa Rosa, somewhere that he had never been, he said.

If only they had not made that comment.

Co-incidentally, and obviously unknown to The Zumstegs at the time was on that exact day, the fact that the Telling family had once again made headlines in the Times newspaper, again for all the wrong reasons. It was something that would happen again on several occasions over the next few years. On this occasion though, it was not Michael that made headlines, but this time it was Lord Samuel Vestey and cousin Edmond. The reason, once again, was tax evasion. They, Vestey had, by this stage, successfully avoided paying income tax for the past 60 years. The Revenue decided that the Vestey family were liable to pay income tax on most recent profits of £4.3 million and surtax on further profits of £7.3 million. In another twist to the story, The Law Lords once again ruled in favour of Vestey as they had done in every effort to force the family to pay tax in the past. They ruled that Vestey was an exception, and they need not pay any tax whatsoever. The result even shocked the resolve of the British tax institution. They were quoted as saying that the shock was, "like an atom bomb."

The result made Vestey and his family most

unpopular with the British taxpayer, with whom there were no exceptions, and at that rate every Mister average, hardworking Brit was liable to hand over 30% of their income or suffer court proceedings. In the first budget after the election victory of Margaret Thatcher in 1979, the top rate was reduced from 83% to 60% and the basic rate from 33% to 30%, but still a sizable chunk of income. The Vestey family had got away with it again. It would not be the last time that a member of the family would spurn the law.

The headlines in The Times that day had been :-
'Richest family in huge tax dodge.
They made £2.3 million in profits
They paid just £10 tax
WHY?'
Why indeed?

If they had seen the headlines, had this story been reported in the USA, it would have meant nothing to the Zumsteg family anyway. Most of the UK knew little or nothing about the vast wealth of this family. The public were unaware who owned the vastly popular Dewhurst chain of butchers, or that wonderful Fray Bentos corned beef brand. Corned beef is salt-cured brisket of beef. The term comes from the treatment of the meat with large-grained rock salt, also called corns of salt. Sometimes, sugar and spices are also added to corned beef recipes as in Fray Bentos. Vestey was far too important to have his dirty UK washing aired in public, after all - or so he thought. Lord Vestey was, and still is, referred to as 'Lord Spam' by those who knew him, or knew of him.

As for as Zumstegs, they would have no idea who the man on the Harley really was for a long time. Maybe they never would really know, certainly not until it was too late.

CHAPTER
SEVEN

LOU AND ELSA ZUMSTEG had moved to the peaceful and pretty hillside area of Santa Rosa four years previously from San Francisco.

How different could two locations be, such a short distance from each other. San Fran was always busy, and like New York, never slept. Busy, vibrant and noisy. Santa Rosa was the mirror opposite. They had made the decision not to move again after the manufacturing business of which Lou was a director, decided to move its operation to 'The windy city', Chicago. Frank Sinatra's it may have been, but Lou's kind of town it was not. He still worked from Santa Rosa, but now he was self-employed, and suited himself when and where he took jobs as a peacemaker for industrial relations.

It suited them both and gave Lou more to concentrate on the loves of his life, motorcycles, Elsa, twin children Erika and Mark, and daughter Monika, but not necessarily in that order. Monika lived and worked in Sacramento, around 120 miles inland from Santa Rosa.

And so, into the life of the Zumsteg family, came Michael Telling. He stayed with them, they expected him to stay overnight, but he ingratiated himself, and clearly was settled in for a while. Lou showed him his extensive motorcycle collection, told then the names he had christened them with individually and the two new best friends climbed aboard their machines and went for a tour of Sonoma Valley.

Sonoma County is a major wine-producing region north of San Francisco. Hundreds of vineyards, ranging from small, family-run estates to international wineries, are set amid its rolling hills and valleys, including Sonoma Valley and Russian River Valley. The region is also home to wilderness areas such as Armstrong Redwoods State Preserve and sandy beaches, many of which frame Bodega Bay.

Having ingratiated himself, after a few days, Telling had outstayed his welcome. He clearly had no intention of leaving, even though Lou had to leave on business. This did not faze Lou, who suggested that Elsa take him on a tour of the many and various wineries in the Valley, just a few miles from their home.

They did just that and Telling said that he wanted to buy some gifts, and one specifically for himself. This gift would feature in my life in the future. Else had knowledge of a shop that serviced local law enforcement officers, and she took Telling there. At that location Michael Telling was able to buy himself a full California Highway

Patrol motor cyclists' uniform, resplendent with helmet, handcuffs and cosh. No checks on the man that made the purchase, in America cash is all that is required.

He made many other purchases over the next few days, and paid for them all on credit card, as noted by Elsa. She had previously noticed his wallet stuffed with $500 Travellers cheques. Elsa was beginning to wonder about the Englishman.

After he had been there for a week, he still seemed to have no plan, nor intention to leave.

He was secretive about himself, but asked numerous questions about Elsa, her children and her family. As for himself, he implied many things, but actually said very little, and skilfully swerved and avoided questions. He did admit to having served in the Australian army in Vietnam as a medic, but avoiding direct answers to anything else. He made her think that he worked for the British government, mentioning 'Whitehall' several times in passing. He stated that he had to telephone London for an extension to his leave. He said no more about it, but Elsa knew what was in 'Whitehall', and asked no more. If he wanted to tell her, and if he was able to do so, she had been sure he would have done so. He enquiring mind was further tormented by an unexpected telephone call to the Zumsteg landline. The official sounding voice identified himself as an official of the Australian Consulate, asking to speak to Michael Telling.

Michael Telling requested some privacy, and Elsa left the room without question, suspecting that the call had something to do with his secret and clearly important job. It all made perfect sense now.

Michael Telling still appeared to have no plan to leave. Lou returned from his business trip and was surprised to see the Brit was still there. The hospitality was wearing a little thin, although the softly spoken Englishman had been no trouble at all. More than that and more importantly, the family liked him.

The only trouble was finding ways to keep him entertained, to find new things to show him, places to take him. Lou had an idea that at the time seemed like a good idea. The idea was to invite Michael Telling to visit their other daughter in Sacramento, to visit Monika Zumsteg. *Really not the best idea he had ever had.*

~~It was an idea that would haunt him for the remainder of his life.~~

CHAPTER
EIGHT

HALF MOON BAY High School is an American public high school located in Half Moon Bay, in San Mateo County, California.

Unlike the United Kingdom, public schools in North America, are generally primary or secondary State schools mandated for or offered to all children without charge, funded in whole or in part by taxation. Half Moon Bay High School's graduating seniors standard assessment test scores have consistently averaged well above the overall California state mean. An overwhelming majority of the school's students matriculate to college upon graduation.

Monika Zumsteg was one such gifted student. Away from school, the young girl was a workaholic. An honour role student, she was never satisfied with anything lower than an A grade – a B+ she considered a failure, but away from her studies and at the same time, she worked for 20 hours in a nursing home, a facility for the residential care of elderly or disabled people. In addition, as a volunteer, she delivered hot meals to the old and vulnerable.

Back at school she played piano, excelled at gymnastics, in particular at figure skating, and had thoughts of Olympic glory, but her main love was for literature and poetry. She left Half Moon Bay High School in 1974, and was certainly alchemically gifted enough for one of the main universities in California, perhaps UCLA in Los Angeles, or Berkeley in San Francisco. Instead she decided at nearer home.

The College of San Mateo is a gateway to higher education leading to university transfer, career preparation and advancement, and professional and personal development, and it was Monika's college of choice. She had intended to continue her education at Notre Dame de Namur University, a private Catholic university in Belmont, California. It is the third oldest college in California and the first college in the state authorized to grant the baccalaureate degree to women. A baccalaureate degree is just another term for a bachelor's degree, a type of undergraduate degree usually awarded after four years of continuous study of a particular subject.

She was expected to go into the field of sports or music, but a summer job as a computer operator enabled her to find her niche in life, and she also excelled at that. She decided against another move of colleges at that time, and decided to continue her part time job, and at the same time to continue with her studies, whilst being able to rent an apartment off campus. She attained a degree in journalism, and she eventually enrolled at Notre Dame de Namur University, and because of her aptitude with, and success with, she had decided that a future in the computer industry was for her. Her job at this time was almost full time, and her studies suffered. It was proving impossible to do both. However, the unshakable and strong young woman was not prepared to give up on her studies, she just decided it would take her more time to attain her goal.

Apart from her tenacity, there was no doubt that she was considered a beautiful young woman. She had auburn hair, and her almost luminous green eyes sparkled under her contact lenses. Her looks did not alter her ambition, to become a computer executive. After all, one day everyone would have their own computer at home – wouldn't they?

The Reynolds and Reynolds Company is a private corporation based in Dayton, Ohio with branches throughout the USA. Its primary business is providing business forms, management software and professional services to car dealerships. Its software is used to manage sales logistics at dealerships. Being posted near to her family home at her own request, Monika commenced her employment with Reynolds and Reynolds as a field agent. Reynolds and Reynolds have been approached for recollections and comments on Monika, and her time with them, but like so many others, they have made no comment.

This work included installing computer systems, and training staff to utilise them to stock check and make accounting much easier within the dealerships. But the ambitious young woman did not have to wait long, as within a year she was promoted to supervisor at Sacramento, a step towards a managerial position, but she could not continue to study part time for her degree course at Notre Dame, and she quit the university.

Young Monika was accepted at California State University, Sacramento to continue her studies and she moved to Sacramento, the city of trees, the state capital of California since 1854. It is also famous for coffee, quoted as the 'world's best cities for coffee lovers' or a city 'that's earned its coffee bragging rights.'

Howsoever it sold itself.

Monika Zumsteg lived there, worked there, socialised there and studied there. Unknown to her, six months later she would meet the man who would eventually change, and ultimately end her youthful and radiant young life.

The man named Michael Henry Maxwell Telling from England.

CHAPTER
NINE

THE BRITISH DO NOT NORMALLY LIKE to outstay their welcome.

Although not the pushy kind, Michael Telling certainly outstayed the warm welcome extended to him by the Zumsteg family in Santa Rosa. Although hints were given, it took time before Telling took the hint and left to accept more hospitality, this time in Sacramento, and this time by their daughter Monika.

By this time, Telling had purchased another new Harley Davidson, the first one had been shipped back to somewhere in England. But before he left, he felt it only fair, he said, to clear the decks so to speak, and to open up about himself to the open armed Zumsteg family.

He had never really spoken about himself, had remained somewhat secretive about his family, his past and his employment. Today he would tell all, or as much as he was permitted to do so, he said. The explanation he gave was not entirely unexpected. The

Zumstegs were by no means stupid people, they had guessed – and guessed correctly. It came as no shock to either of them but it did explain a lot. The call from the Australian High Commission had been an obvious clue as to the Brit's true identity.

He told them that he lived in Torquay, Devon a seaside resort in the south west of England around 100 miles from Poole. Royal Marines Base Poole is a British naval base located in Hamworthy, a suburb of Poole, Dorset, England on the Poole Harbour and is the centre for Special Boat Service activities also known as the SBS, the elite commandos of the Royal Navy. They are the naval equivalent of the better-known SAS, the Special Air Service, a branch of the British army. Most of the operations conducted by the SBS are highly classified, and are rarely commented on by the British government or the UK Ministry of Defence due to their sensitive and secretive nature, and to protect the identity of the elite troops.

In Torquay he rented a cottage along with two Royal Marine commandos, he said. They all travelled around the world frequently, and saw little of each other.

He stated that the Official Secrets Act prevented him from explaining his work in detail, much of it was extremely sensitive after all.

The icing on the cake, and the true reason for his enforced leave of absence was that he had recently been in Iran. Presidential elections were held for the first time in Iran on 25 January 1980, one year after the Iranian Revolution when the Council of the Islamic Revolution was in power. Abolhassan Banisadr was elected president with 76% of the vote. Telling hinted that he had some involvement, but that things had gone badly wrong and lives were lost.

As a punishment, he was required to take an enhanced leave of absence, by his seniors in MI6, and because of that he had decided to visit The States, San Francisco, to buy a Harley or two and to see California.

The quiet young Englishman was a spy! *That explained everything.* They were sure that he would like their daughter Monika, when he saw her later in Sacramento.

CHAPTER
TEN

LAKE TAHOE IS a large freshwater lake in the Sierra Nevada of the United States of America. It straddles the state line between California and Nevada, west of Carson City. It is exactly 123 miles from Sacramento.

It is a major tourist attraction in both Nevada and California. It is also home to winter sports, summer outdoor recreation, and scenery enjoyed throughout the year. The climate is odd. There can be sheet ice and snow at the summit of the mountains, and the roads could be treacherous, and there would, at the same time, be beautiful hot sun in the town. Snow and ski resorts are a significant part of the area's economy and reputation. The Nevada side also offers several lake-side casino resorts.

It is to one of these resorts that Monika Zumsteg and Michael Telling went the day after he arrived in Sacramento. Monika had won an all expenses paid break for two at Harveys.

Oddly enough, I was also passing through Lake Tahoe at the same time on a family holiday. I was driving from Utah to San Francisco. The snow and ice were so severe that a car in front of me, travelling too fast, slid under a lorry going downhill, the car slid under the lorry taking the top from the car and decapitating the driver. An odd sight to greet my arrival in Lake Tahoe!

The hotel named Harveys, situated at Highway 50 at Stateline Avenue, is a 4/5 star resort, and it was the very first casino hotel built on the South Shore of the mile high resort. It opened in 1944, and the massive casino boasts 'over 88,000 square feet of gaming space that includes 'more than 1,200 of the most exciting slot machines'.

Prior to leaving, he had impressed both Monika and her room-mate, Samantha Hynes with a huge purchase of roses for Monika and carnations for Samantha. They both found him to be an engaging young man. At Harveys he lavished attention and money on Monika. Fresh flowers every day, and the well-travelled and well-spoken Englishman was unlike any of his American contempories. He was sophisticated, and he agreed with Monika on everything, even equality in the workplace for women.

The break was a success, and it was clear that they were both falling for each other. The only issue that Monika had was his apparent generosity, continually wanting to buy her gifts. This continued when they returned to Sacramento. Monika had taken few things there from home, but one thing that she did take was an article of great sentimental value. It was an old black and white TV set, a family tv set. When Monika returned home from work the next day, Telling had replaced it with a huge colour TV, and trashed the old family set. His actions in getting rid of her things upset and annoyed Monika.

Despite the upset, Monika did admit to her friend and flatmate that she was falling for the Englishman, even though he did not fit in with either her plans for education, or work.

Oh, how things would have been so different had they never met, never fallen for each other. I believe that Telling craved attention and love that he had not been shown as a child. Monika had shown him the missing affection.

But Monika was more independent, she was a young woman that knew her own mind – or so she thought.

CHAPTER
ELEVEN

MONIKA WAS A PRETTY LADY, and one who was popular with men.

She made it abundantly clear up until this point that the most important thing in her life was her career. She had plans. Marriage and maybe children came after that. Monika was her own woman, and a woman that would make her own way. She had been virtually stalked by a doctor, a dentist – both of whom wanted to marry her, a UASF sergeant, a restaurant owner, and many other men that she met locally, mostly whilst out with Samantha at the no longer there, Mills Station Bar, a country and western hangout in Sacramento. Monika seemed to gravitate to the bad boys, the ones with a past – with something to hide, or something to prove. Maybe she thought she could change them, maybe she did change some of them. She liked a challenge.

That was, until she met the charming and over generous Michael Telling. Then things changed, and she started to change her mind about many things. She would certainly get her challenge.

Monika and Samantha entertained a colleague from work and his partner, and invited them for dinner. Michael joined the party. When the conversation came around to the inevitable – 'what do you do for work?', Michael lied again. The correct answer would have been, "I don't work. I am so rich that I will never work". Instead he came out with the old favourite, the answer that could not, should not be questioned. He said, once again that he worked for the British Government, that his work was secret and covered by the Official Secrets Act, and that he could not go into detail. Suffice it to say that he had a part in the Iranian hostage siege in Tehran recently, that some things had gone badly wrong, and that he was currently on an enforced term of leave from work.

The guests believed him. Michael Telling was most believable, why would anyone lie about such things to make them look important, after all? In an act, so unlike any police officer, soldier or spy, he thought that if he produced the revolver that he had it would convince then more. And indeed, it did. No more needed to be said.

The romance was brief, very brief, and Michael Telling purchased two first class air tickets to Bermuda, and persuaded Monika to accompany him. They left a couple of days later.

They stayed at the 5 star Rosewood hotel in Tuckers Point Drive, Hamilton. Telling proposed marriage that night in a restaurant overlooking the Atlantic – the view by way of the infinity pool. Monika did not accept immediately, saying that she needed time to think, as her plans had not included marriage up until now. Michael took this to be a positive thing, and the next day he purchased an expensive ring that he said he would keep until she accepted.

The trip back to Sacramento was via San Francisco, the city that Monika knew well. She showed him the old area, the Victorian houses that she loved so much. Telling said that he would buy her one if she accepted his proposal. This surprised her, as the cost at that time was well over $150,000 starting price. As of 2020, the starting prices are around $5 million.

When she returned home and returned to work, her life got even more complicated. She was offered the promotion that she so wanted, Reynolds and Reynolds fist ever female regional co-ordinator.

Telling moved in with Monika and said that he could probably extend his leave if she wished. Monika had a lot of decisions to make. Marriage and a move to England or promotion and stay in the States.

What Monika did not know at this stage was that Telling was still married and had a child, and could not legally marry her anyway. She also knew nothing about his background and his obvious considerable wealth. But she did know that he was a spy and ex elite soldier who worked for the British Government at least.

Even Michael Telling would have to tell the truth, or at least part of it eventually, wouldn't he?

CHAPTER
TWELVE

THE SAN FERNANDO Valley is an urbanised valley in Los Angeles County, California, in the Los Angeles metropolitan area, defined by the mountains of the Transverse Ranges circling it.

Home to 1.77 million people then, it is north of the larger, more populous Los Angeles Basin. It was one of the poorer districts of the city, mostly housing Mexican immigrants at this time, but Monika loved it there and looked forward to moving there. She had rented an apartment there. She also loved her new regional service co-ordinator position at Reynolds and Reynolds.

She confided that she was no longer sure about her acceptance of Michael's proposal of marriage. She was having fun. She really did not want to leave her new base, she did not want to leave her parents or her twin siblings and she really did not want to move to England. That was not her destiny, her clear way through life that she had mapped out. Monika was twenty-four years old, and she had everything to live for. She was just unsure if that everything included Michael Telling.

But fate has its own way of deciding one's future. And fate decided that Telling was so infatuated, when he had completed his secret mission in London, he unexpectedly arrived in Los Angeles deciding to surprise her. And surprise her he certainly did.

She showed him her chosen apartment, and Telling objected to her choice of accommodation. He told her that the area was unsafe – which it certainly was. He had made the decision to pay rent on a better class apartment in a better class area, with better class security, but Monika objected.

She did not need his help, and would pay for herself until, and if they were married. But the smooth-talking Englishman talked her around, and he agreed to pay half the rent and half the expenses as he would live there when he visited Los Angeles. He moved in with Monika, continued to lie about himself, and once again omitted to tell about his wife and child back in England.

He did, however, share more details of his top-secret military background. He bored her with his knowledge of the SAS from its formation. He could tell her that in many ways, the formation of the SAS was an accident. It was the brainchild of one officer, a man called David Stirling, who was a commander in the Middle East in 1940. He told her of their early operations in North Africa, the Greek Islands, and the Invasion of Italy. They then returned to the United Kingdom and were formed into a brigade with two

British, two French and one Belgian regiment. She had been unaware of it until then, and unaware of the recent Iranian embassy siege in London which received little publicity in the States, although naturally he said that he had some involvement in that mission.

He said that he had completed many missions overseas in Vietnam, Iran and Northern Ireland and Australia – not to boast, but to name just a few. One thing that he made very clear was that by telling her this, he was in breach of the Official Secrets Act that he was bound by, and liable to imprisonment, and as a result she was now also bound by it now and bound to a code of total secrecy.

They moved to the apartment in Van Neys, a better area, and one described as, 'The international epicentre of entertainment and home of the Dodgers, Lakers, Kings, Rams, Angels, Chargers, LAFC, Clippers, Galaxy..... we also have wildfires, earthquakes, movie stars, television studios, music, world-class food, beaches, mountains, traffic jams, museums and theme parks.

The expensive gifts that she did not want or need, and also the lies continued, and Monika was becoming increasing uncertain about this man, the man who never asked prices of anything, just paid by card, and additionally uncertain of what she really wanted. Wanted from him, and indeed wanted from her life. He was worse than reckless with money, and a furious argument ensued when Michael invited a friend to dinner, a Brit and an ex-marine, he had said, though the man was clearly desolate and most unlike any soldier that she had ever met.

The two men swapped war stories. Monika thought that Telling was, at best, exaggerating or bending the truth, even if he was anything like the hero that he made himself out to be, and had really done all those things that are normally only seen on film by celluloid heroes. Amazingly, after the 'friend' had admired his watch, a top of the range expensive Rolex, Michael took it off and gave it to him! This was a trait of Arab kings and queens, and a well-known ruse to get property from them. In that culture, they are considered to be rude if they did give it to the person who has openly admired it. Not a trait of an Englishman who worked as a spy for the government, surely.

Monika thought him to be insane, and explained that people do not do that kind of thing in real life, or in the life that they live in. Telling's attitude was that it did not matter and that he could afford many more like that. Real life and living in the real world seemed alien to him, even at that stage of his life. Monika was furious at his attitude and also at his crass, glaring, undisguised stupidity. She threatened to call the wedding off.

The next day, Telling was found in a diabetic coma and near death. He had 'forgotten' to take his insulin. Had he forgotten, or, like as a spoilt child, and now a spoilt adult, maybe it was the way of getting what he wanted, a way of stamping his proverbial feet. Either way it worked.

Some truth came out of it though. Telling was

sulking in his hospital room, refusing to speak to anyone. Monika said to him that she should call his mother. He was, after all, in intensive care, and could have died if Monika had not found him.

That broke his silence. He told her not to make the call, and that his mother was a bitch who cared nothing for him and never had. He said that she had shunned him from birth. He hated her.

The next day, Telling left the hospital. The bill for the private treatment had been a staggering $10000 – equivalent to around $35000 today, and payable before he left. He assured the disbelieving staff that someone would pay it, turned his back on the staff, walked away, and left the hospital and flew back to England.

Shortly afterwards, he telephoned Monika and lied that his boss in the government would not allow him any more leave, and he could not, at least now, return to America.

He begged her to come to England, where they could make plans, and look for a nice expensive house to live in. She had no wish to go to England, then or later actually, and as they were to be married in the cathedral at Santa Rosa, there was much to do, and only a few months to organise such a grand affair.

And then she capitulated, surrendered to Michael Telling's will. She quit her job, and flew to London. He met her at London airport.

If only she knew what awaited her, the intelligent American woman would never have got on that aircraft.

CHAPTER
THIRTEEN

AND SO, the California girl arrived in England.

With the exception of Michael Telling she knew no-one and was unfamiliar with England and its protocol. But she fitted in very well and adapted to her new country.

The happy-ish couple went to live in Tunbridge Wells, now known as Royal Tunbridge Wells. The prefix Royal dates to 1909, when King Edward VII granted the town its official 'Royal' title to celebrate its popularity over the years among members of the royal family and the British aristocracy. They even seemed content for a while. They looked forward to their wedding and started looking for a home.

On a visit to Lou and Elsa Zumsteg, Telling had revealed his ancestry to Monika's parents, and the fact that he was an heir to a vast fortune. Also, he said that the current Lord Vestey, Samuel had not only taken the title, but also inherited a vast fortune, a huge share of a trust worth billions of pounds, established by his great-grandfather.

He explained that he actually received a monthly stipendiary, and that all bills incurred by him were also paid. He explained that their daughter would never have money worries and that the trust would buy them any house they wished after they were married.

He admitted to insinuating rather than lying about his position in the SAS and British Intelligence, being a spy. He said that Monika knew and considered that he had lied to her parents.

He also admitted to being married, having started divorce proceedings. He explained not having told Monika immediately about his current marriage, of his inherited wealth because he did not want it to turn her away from him.

He had also admitted to not having been in the military, or having served in Vietnam, saying that he was unable to attain his dream of military service due to diabetes. He begged for their forgiveness and sought their help in persuading Monika to still marry him, even though the divorce was taking longer than expected, and they may not be able to meet the September date that had been set for the wedding. Monika was still furious at the lies that had been told, but had, for the moment forgiven him enough to still marry him.

The full confession had taken place over a two-week period.

Monika and the Zumstegs were impressed that

Michael had the courage to own up. He said that he had told them everything.

The big cathedral wedding was cancelled in favour of a smaller registry office wedding in England, if it was still what Monika wanted.

Telling made up, or tried to make up, for his deceit to Monika and to her parents, by purchasing a pre-wedding gift for Monika. It was her dream car, a beautiful white Pontiac Firebird sports car, paid for on American Express, paid for from the vast Vestey trust fund. It would be shipped to England.

'American Express sir? That will do nicely'

CHAPTER
FOURTEEN

MICHAEL TELLING WAS CALLED to London.

He was told, he said, that the divorce was proceeding and that he could expect a decree absolute by the end of the year. Then they could get married immediately and look for a suitable house to live in, just as soon as Mr Brown agreed.

Monika was given a new Volkswagen Golf to drive around in, while waiting for her Pontiac Firebird to arrive in the country.

He, Telling, also told her that she was required to go to London, to sign a prenup, a prenuptial agreement. This is a written contract entered into by a couple prior to marriage that enables them to select and control many of the legal rights they acquire upon marrying, and what happens when their marriage eventually ends by death or divorce. It also enables one of the parties to surrender all rights to the others property. It was a new thing for the family solicitors, as Telling's previous wife had not been required to sign one and was now entitled to the home that they once briefly shared in Devon, and to an income for life.

Monika had no interest in his family money, or his property, or the house that the trust would buy them, she said. And so, she would sign the agreement, and signed away all rights to anything that Michael Telling owned.

Through the enhanced newspaper coverage of The Vestey tax situation, Monika learnt a little about her new family. Michael had not shared the information with her.

Samuel Vestey, Baron Samuel George Armstrong, was the head of the family and the empire. He had been educated at Eton and had been an officer in the army. He owned Stowell Park, a 6,000-acre, seven square mile, historic agricultural and sporting estate in the Cotswold Hills, Gloucestershire, England. The estate includes the village of Yanworth. The main house is a Grade II listed building and surrounded by extensive parkland, a mill, and church. The landscaped park is listed Grade II on the Register of Historic Parks and Gardens. The house was built around 1600 for Robert Atkinson, on the site of a previous house. It has 65 rooms and the value was inestimable. It was reported in the newspapers that he was divorcing his current wife. The grounds for divorce were simple. His current wife was unable to supply him with a male heir to his title.

He was, and is, friends with Charles, Prince of Wales, and a member of Charles's Highgrove polo team, as was Samuel's younger brother Mark Vestey. Mark was a glamourous figure in the polo world, even though at age 41 he was left paralyzed from the chest down following a hunting accident. He also lived on the Stowell estate. He had played polo at a professional level, and had previously represented England and won the Gold Cup on five occasions. He ran the empires South African meat farms.

Samuel's first cousin also ran the business empire from London. He had also been to Eton, had been high sheriff and deputy Lord Lieutenant of the City of London Yeomanry, master of the hounds, chairman of the Blue Star shipping line, and the owner of the 150 square mile Assynt estate in the West of Scotland. A famous quote about Assynt is, 'Every self-respecting billionaire should own their own country estate – it's the ultimate prestige purchase'.

And so, little by little, with the help of the British press, Monika learnt more of her soon to be family. She was terrified at the prospect of joining such an infamous family.

In her adopted country, she saw fox hunting. Fox hunting is an activity involving the tracking, chase and, if caught, the killing of a fox, traditionally a red fox, by trained foxhounds or other scent hounds, and a group of unarmed followers led by a master of foxhounds, who follow the hounds on foot or on horseback.

It appealed to the girl from California, and she asked Michael if he would buy her a horse. He agreed. He said he would buy her anything she ever wanted, including a house of her choice.

Monika disliked London. It was too crowded. Tunbridge Wells was too big. Monika decided that she wanted to live in the country. She started her horse-riding lessons on her new horse, and the couple looked for a suitable home for a soon to be married couple.

They were both called to London, to see Mr Brown. There were no rules, no budget he said. Whatever they wanted, the trust would pay for, he said. This man, the Vestey financial adviser, Edward Brown, normally bowler hatted, interviewed, interrogated Monika. He clearly thought her too young for Michael. Michael had already made one mistake by marrying a young girl and having a family. He warned that the Vestey way was to keep a low profile. Nothing too flashy, nothing that would show out. Live inconspicuously, no flashy cars. No extravagances, spend in moderation.

The couple were to be given an allowance, and at the end of each month, credit card receipts were to be submitted and would be paid. Travel would be first class, through the family owned Blue Star Line. There were no budgets to adhere to, no real limits to stay within, but the Vestey way was 'frugality and discretion in all things'. At least outwardly, that is.

It was explained that if the marriage failed, she would be looked after financially for the remainder of her life, as would any child or children they may have, but by signing the documents she would have no other lien on anything owned by the Vestey's or Michael Telling. In retrospect she was literally signing her life away. And so, she agreed and she did sign the documents, witnessed by and countersigned by Mr Brown.

They would be contacted by estate agents, and helped to buy a home. Negotiations would take place on their behalf once there was a shortlist, and a suitable property purchased for them. It would be paid for, and owned by the Vestey Trust.

There was one such a property available in a village on the outskirts of West Wycombe, Buckinghamshire. It was a beautiful property named Lambourne House in Radnage near to High Wycombe.

CHAPTER
FIFTEEN

FROM THEN ON, there was increasing violence in the relationship.

It continued, and at Christmas that year, 1981, the festivities were not a joyous event for the couple. In one of the many arguments, Telling punched Monika in the face. He blackened her eye. The reason was that she moaned too much, but mostly because the Californian did not like warm drinks, and had dared to ask for ice!

Aunt Liz had confided in Monika regarding his formative years, the lack of love from his mother, and the problems with tantrums, violence and damage that he had caused. Also, the hospitalisation and the treatment that he was given for his mental illness, although in those days he was considered more of a 'troubled child.'

Things quickly escalated. The violence became more severe. Monika confided in Elsa about the previous episode in Tunbridge, where he had destroyed the bannister. After that episode, he had smashed windows and chairs. He had knocked Monika to the floor and held the gun to her head, threatening to kill her. Naturally, she was frightened for her life. But still she married him a short while later. She had made the excuse of a blood sugar imbalance. *Another excuse for the coward who hit a woman.*

On Saturday 23rd January 1982, Telling and Monika attended a formal wedding of a relative of his in Guildford, Surrey. Telling drove them in his highly tuned Mini Cooper. It had been the kind of wedding that Monika had wanted, expected, and an argument ensued. Monika was still enjoying herself, and drinking. Some say steadily, Telling said heavily, too much. He noticed that the wife of one of his other cousins was wearing a mink coat. Telling considered that to be unfair, as Monika did not have one. Telling set off to find Mr Brown, to remonstrate with the financier.

Monika attempted to stop him, and he said that they were leaving. He was leaving, and Monika was coming with him. He was in a blind rage. Monika refused, and said that she was staying.

Telling went to the car park, to the Mini Cooper, and sat there waiting. He waited until Monika left, and got into a car. Telling smashed into the back of it, backed up and smashed into it again, causing severe damage to both vehicles. Clearly Monika was once again terrified, but Telling backed up once more and smashed into the car again.

I believe that his attitude was 'I am a Vestey. We are untouchable. Money can put anything right'. And in some ways, he was absolutely correct.

Telling then drove himself back to Lambourne House. He later said to me that he drove back flat out, around 130 miles an hour. I doubted it. Back in Guildford, shocked wedding guests had already called the Surrey police.

The Surrey police called Thames Valley police, and Thame police station, the police station that covered a huge 350 square mile area, including the area of Lambourne House and its grounds.

On that night, I was the duty CID officer at Thame police station. I received an order, on behalf of the police in Guildford, to attend Lambourne House, and to arrest Michael Telling for criminal damage.

The outcome would be somewhat different to that.

CHAPTER
SIXTEEN

CALLS ABOUT TELLING came into the police station at Thame.

The first call said to take care, as he was thought to have a shotgun. The second call changed that. He was thought to illegally possess a powerful handgun. There was only one person who could have given them that information.

I was then a firearms trained police officer, authorised to carry a gun, and to use it if absolutely necessary. Despite what is broadly said, and thought, police are taught to shoot to kill, or they were back then. A wounded man can shoot back.

To carry a firearm on an operation, one had to have the authority of a senior officer. The duty senior officer at Thame that night was a woman, Chief Inspector Jill Read. Miss Read was a graduate entry to the police force, and as such was rapidly promoted through the ranks to her present level. Her degree was in religion, possibly not the most useful in these circumstances.

I made a request to carry a gun, and explained the circumstances to her. She refused my request, saying," I will come with you. We will deal with it. No need for firearms".

And so we left the police station and travelled to Lambourne house. Unarmed, and unsure what we would find when we got there.

When we arrived at Lambourne House, it was late at night, the Mini was there. I think to say that it looked all the worse for its ordeal would be a fair assessment. It would be accurate to say that in a contest of two, the Mini had been the runner up.

The lights were on throughout the house, and there was a small fire in one of the outbuildings.

What happened next happened exactly as described here. In a previous book about Telling, up to his next conviction, it skated over what actually happened next and subsequently. The author never met Telling, nor Monika and the book is based on supposition and rumour. He refused to speak to me, or to change his account, even though he has been requested to do so by Monika's family.

And so, the small fire in the outhouse consisted of Monika's photos, certificates, paperwork and other personal items. It had been set by Telling in a rage. I managed to extinguish the fire, and knocked on the kitchen door.

What happened next was something that I was not prepared for. It was getting late, my shift was nearly over, and frankly I just wanted to get home. I had an early start the next morning, a trip to the north of

England to arrest someone else. It had been arranged with a northern police force in advance, and I was to go with my detective sergeant.

My shift was nowhere ending at that stage.

CHAPTER
SEVENTEEN

I KNOCKED ON THE DOOR, and I identified us as both as local police officers.

A male that I now know to be Michael Telling shouted from inside. "I have locked the door, you can't come in until I speak to my solicitor, our family solicitor. He will know what I should do".

This stumped me for a few seconds.

I said, "are you Michael Telling". He admitted that he was. He appeared to be in an excitable mood.

I said, "No problem Michael, sounds like a good idea. Get him on the phone, and when you have, why not let me speak to him? I can explain why I am here, and my intentions".

Telling agreed and did just that. He contacted his solicitor by telephone and the conversation lasted a short time. I then heard him unlocking the door.

I entered Lambourne House and met Michael Telling for the first time. I seem to remember that the kitchen connected with another room that contained seating, settees. I took the telephone handset from him and spoke to the solicitor. I had a feeling of unease as Telling walked away into the room containing the seating. I said to Chief Inspector Read, " There is something very wrong here. Go to the car and radio for some assistance".

It should be noted and remembered that mobile telephones were not available, and police radio communications were less than perfect at that time. The request may not have worked, but better to try, I thought. Better to be safe than sorry. Safety in numbers and all that.

The Chief Inspector said, "I can't do that. He locked the door behind me". Really?

I said to the voice at the other end of the telephone, a man who identified himself as Kenneth Dimmick "I can't speak now, something is very wrong here. I will speak to you later, but I will be arresting your client and taking him to Aylesbury". Despite his protest I then cut off the call, but he did say that he was the solicitor for the powerful Vestey family. It meant nothing for me at that time. I went into the room off the kitchen, and saw Telling stood next to a settee. I spoke to him. Firstly, asked him if I knew why I was there. He said he did, something about causing a bit of damage by mistake. He was jittery, excitable.

He reached under one of the cushions on the nearest settee. I saw the glint of a pistol barrel facing in my direction. At this point I would say that the firearms training that I received was superb. The training taught you how to shoot, told you when to shoot, and for sure after four weeks, you knew beyond a doubt if you had the mental capacity to shoot – most importantly. If the instructors did not feel that you could do so, you were not authorised to carry a gun.

What it never did teach you was how to react in a situation where someone stood next to you is holding a gun and the business end is facing you. To this day, I don't think anything really can. I believe that the natural instinct to survive kicks in. The question I have asked myself so many times is, "If I had been issued a gun when I asked, would I have used it. Would I have shot and killed Michael Telling?" My answer is, "Yes, I think I would have done".

But I did not have a weapon, and clearly, he did.

It would be foolish of me to say exactly what happened next, and I have no intention of doing so. I have no recollection what I said, but I know I saw black, the next stage after seeing red. It has only happened that one time in my life.

Hostile people have hostile thoughts; hostile thoughts are implicitly associated with the colour red, and therefore hostile people are biased to see this colour more frequently. If you are angrier and less hostile, you see the colour black.

It would be safe to say that Michael Telling found himself quickly on the floor, I hit him- hard, and I took possession of his Colt Python pistol, turned on him in the most vicious way. The weapon unloaded by chance not by design. Fate had decided that. Maybe the wrong decision. It had six dum- dum bullets in the cylinder, I found when I made it safe.

I formally arrested Telling. Behind the settee was a Colt AR15, the civilian version or the M16 military machine gun. This gun was also loaded and cocked. The magazine contained 29 rounds and one in the chamber. Here were hundreds of rounds of ammunition, spare magazines, speed loaders, and many military field rations. Enough to start a small war, I thought. Ironically, the ration packs were manufactured by Vestey Foods.

And so, my prisoner was taken to Aylesbury police station. I do remember that he said on several occasions how grateful he was that I had not shot him when I could have done so. He had not realised that the fact I had not was down to circumstance, and chance. Had I done so, other people would have lived, and many people's lives would be so very different, including mine.

But as I did not, with a night spent at Aylesbury police station, I had an appointment to keep the next day. That appointment meant a long drive and another arrest in another police area, following a shower and a change of clothes. Telling was going nowhere.

That completed, I returned to Aylesbury. There I met Monika for the first time. She was a pretty lady, but very upset, very tearful. She seemed like a person who needed to speak, to unburden herself.

She told me many things, but they mostly concerned the things that Telling had said and had done. She was unhappy in her short marriage. Telling was unpredictable, sometimes childlike. He would alternately fly into rages then into fits of tears.

Most importantly, on several occasions he had held guns to her head and threatened to kill her. With the illegally imported Coly Python cannon, he had held it to her head and played Russian roulette.

Russian roulette is a lethal game of chance in which a player places a single round in a revolver, spins the cylinder, places the muzzle against their head, and pulls the trigger in hopes that the loaded chamber does not align with the primer percussion mechanism and the explode the bullet. Except that Telling held the revolver, spun the chamber, and pulled the trigger.

During one of my interviews I was called away. The duty superintendent wanted to see me – now. That man was uniform Superintendent Maurice Caro.

I knew Mister Caro quite well. Up until recently he had been a detective chief inspector, and the senior detective who had recommended me for CID. Up until he spoke to me then, I had absolute respect for him. That was about to lessen. Telling had done that to me. Things would never be the same. The story that sounded like fiction was fact, total fact. I went into his office on the first floor. He told me to sit and to tell me about the arrest. And tell him I did. "Bullshit", he said. "Things don't happen in the real world like that".

I replied, "Sir. You know I have great respect for you. But you are very wrong, totally wrong. That is exactly what happened, what I will say in court." I then stood and left the room, waiting for repercussions.

Those repercussions were many and varied. Firstly, Telling was charged with the firearms offences and criminal damage, and released from custody. Telling immediately booked himself into a private mental clinic.

CHAPTER
EIGHTEEN

THERE IS no doubt at all, and it has never been contested, that Michael Telling was a wife beater.

Shortly after his arrest, and whilst on bail, on 14th February Monika had purchased an air purifier for his CB room. Telling was a chain smoker, and the acrid smell had penetrated the very fabric of Lambourne House, and in particular, his games room, his CB room. He punched her in the face, blackening her eye. That was the proverbial straw that broke the back of Monika's resolve to save the marriage. The arrest and trial had been an embarrassment at best, and further alienated the couple from the rest of civilisation. She told him that she was leaving him.

Michael Telling, in his usual dramatic act, took some barbiturates and fell sleep. He had written Monika a note. It said that he had killed himself with the tablets because he could not face life without her. He had also written a note to Monika's father, Lou. In it he admitted having hit her on numerous occasions, but as was usual, blamed her.

She was drinking too much, used words he did not understand, and criticised him constantly. She was constantly threatening him with the police, and time in prison should he get another conviction. He could not take imprisonment, or life without Monika, and that was the reason for his suicide.

His suicide attempt and the coma that the tablets had induced meant that Telling was rushed to High Wycombe General hospital. When Monika attended, she confided in a, and reached out to a nurse about his violence and her very real fear for her life. The nurse did not believe her, and later described her as 'an intoxicated and obnoxious American with a black eye, who constantly argued with her semi-conscious husband'. As Telling was regaining consciousness, he made it very clear that he did not want to stay. He fought against the staff. Monika had begged them not to release him. They took no notice of her, and she ran out of the hospital in tears.

The hospital did not report her fears to the police station, only hundreds of yards from the hospital. They had not believed her fears.

Monika drove the 200-mile journey from Buckinghamshire to Torquay, a town by the sea in south Devon, England. It has an unusually mild climate and this has made it a popular place for holidays since the early 19th century. It was also where Michael Telling's first wife and son lived, following the separation and divorce, in the property named Fir Tree Lodge, a detached house with five bedrooms and five bathrooms paid for by the Vestey Trust because there had been no prenup before Alison, previously Alison Webber had married Michael Telling in 1978.

The two women got on well, and discovered that their time with Telling had been an only too familiar story. Happiness, depression, childish sulking and mental foot stamping to get his own way, obsession with Harleys, guns, police and uniforms, and lies. Lies about his past, and violence.

Meanwhile Telling had discharged himself from Wycombe General Hospital. He had left in a hospital gown and hailed a cab. Expecting Monika to pay the fare, he was shocked to find the house locked.

He broke in by smashing a window. The cab driver went to a neighbour and suggested that the police should be called. The neighbour recognised Telling's description and suggested that it was no crime for a man to break into his own home. But inside Lambourne House, Telling was destroying it from the inside out. Smashing and destroying everything he encountered. Nothing was safe. He destroyed clocks, settees and the kitchen. Thousands of pounds of damage had been caused.

It also caused another coma in Telling. Monika had already learned that Telling had discharged himself from hospital, and telephoned Lambourne House. There was no reply. She called other people, but again got no reply.

A local man named Frank Collier, a gardener inherited from the previous owner had also been called. Michael considered him a friend. He did not have many. I am aware that this 'friend', was light fingered, and was once caught out and replaced the liberated items, and Telling never knew.

Collier had a key, and went to Lambourne, a short distance from Bledlow where he lived. Having let himself in, he found the devastation caused by Telling, and the man himself unconscious. He called an ambulance. When Telling had discharged himself, walked out of Wycombe General hospital, his diabetes had not been stabilised after his failed suicide attempt. Had Collier not found him when he did, he would have died within hours.

This man was very much like a cat. He had already lost two of his nine lives in a matter of weeks.

CHAPTER NINETEEN

AFTER MY INTERVIEWS WITH TELLING, which would span the next two months, and interviews with Monika, it would not have taken Sherlock Holmes to see where this was heading.

I considered Michael Telling to be a deluded and very dangerous man.

Monika still cared for Michael Telling, and on receiving the news of his coma, immediately drove back from Torquay and to Wycombe General Hospital once again. Reports describe her as under the influence of alcohol.

The symptoms of the effects of alcohol, and shock look similar. Was Monika under the influence of alcohol, or was she more likely in shock? She had just been told that her abusive husband would have surely died had it not been for her actions. Shock is a human response. Rapid pulse, rapid breathing, anxiousness or agitation are all signs of shock – and signs of excess alcohol.

Monika called Mr. Brown, begging for help for Michael. She feared for his own safety and for the safety of others. She also spoke to the Vestey solicitor, Kenneth Dimmick. Dimmick made the necessary arrangements on behalf of the family.

St Andrew's Hospital is a large private facility in Northampton, which provided private psychiatric services for those with the ability to pay for it. I visited there when Telling had hospitalised himself at this time, after I arrested him and prior to his trial.

The entrance is via a large Georgian mansion, with newer, private outbuildings for patients, inmates. Literature for the facility boasts, 'We care for some of the most clinically complex patients in the mental health system, people who could not, in many cases, be treated elsewhere. Many of our patients have been in the criminal justice system and are some of the most vulnerable people being treated anywhere in the health service'. People such as Michael Telling, clinically complex people who could afford to have the best treatment that money could buy. The hospital with over 100 acres of grounds, and its own golf course, opened in 1838 - with the hospital offering 'humane' care to the mentally ill. St Andrew's was one of four Registered Psychiatric Hospitals that chose not to join the National Health Service in 1948, and one of the most exclusive and expensive, anywhere.

It was another straw that may have broken Monika's back. What it did though was to give her the impetus to actually leave him, leave England, and return to America and to the bosom of her family.

It has been said that Monika got drunk on the

flight, took sleeping tablets and assaulted a customs officer at Boston airport. She was detained and taken to a hospital where she was strapped to a bed.

She was clearly not a violent person, or a threat to anyone. The severity or otherwise of her actions can be summarised as minor at worse, as Monika was immediately released and given a ride to the airport, and given a complimentary flight to San Francisco by the airline TWA. Maybe her threats to sue for unlawful detention and false imprisonment had something to do with these reactions.

CHAPTER
TWENTY

MONIKA WAS able to vent her fears and frustration over a coffee with her mother.

She told her of the violence, and what she had learnt about Michael's childhood and he mental issues. She explained about her detention at Boston, and her very real fears for the future. When her father Lou, arrived back home, he also listened to his daughters fears, and he was also aware that she also had issues. Monika was drinking too much alcohol, and she realised so.

At 3076 Myrtledale Rd, Calistoga, Califonia is a private alcohol rehab centre named Duffy's Napa Valley Rehab. It was to this facility that Monika went the next day. The Foundational Program is a 30-day residential treatment program intended to help people who are struggling with alcohol disorders, and it was this programme that Monika was signed up for.

Monika completed the course, and left sober and dried out. Lou was to hold her hand through the nest stages in his daughter's rehabilitation. Lou had been, was and alcoholic. He had accepted that much and had sought help from Alcoholics Anonymous. There raison d'etra was to, 'stay sober and help other alcoholics achieve sobriety.' For some people like Lou Zumsteg, it had become a mission. A mission to save the daughter that he loved.

Back in England the stay at St. Andrews had been approved by the police, Telling was still on bail for the firearms offences. He was very verbal about his thoughts regarding this, the police, and the treatment that he had been given.

No regrets, no humility. He had done nothing wrong, he thought. He considered that I had been wrong to take his guns, his property. He was a rich man, why shouldn't he have guns or anything else if he wanted them. He was a Vestey. When the judge knew exactly who he was, all charges would be withdrawn. A man in his position would never go to prison, and at the very worst he would receive a small fine. It was only money, and the judge may have to keep up the appearance of propriety after all.

He wrote to Monika telling her his plans to get fit by taking martial arts and swimming lessons at St. Andrews. He clearly received no reply – Monika was otherwise engaged. This prompted daily telephone calls with demands to speak to Monika, and daily gifts sent to her. When he received no joy this way, he decided to communicate with Lou Zumsteg, telling him how well he was doing at St. Andrews. He also told him that Lambourne was being put back together, and his hopes for the future. He honestly believed that all that had gone before could be put behind them and they could start again because, and that they had so much to look forward to, he was fit, slim and cured of anything that may have been wrong before. There was just this minor court case to deal with, but that was nothing really.

Lou Zumsteg accompanied Monika back to England and to Lambourne house for her interview for university at Oxford, and to start her with Alcoholics Anonymous UK. She wanted to help Michael with his recovery, she had decided.

Telling's calls to America had become more frantic. He accused the family of lying to him, and threatened to commit suicide if Monika did not return. She had spoken to him on the telephone and explained her absence. Because she had stopped drinking, she believed that she could be a better person, and agreed to return.

Back in Northampton, Telling was returning to his old ways. He was variously described as aggressive, rude and disruptive to staff and patients. His attitude frustrated the staff. He constantly bragged about his status, money, his beautiful wife, and his daring military adventures whilst in the SAS and MI5. He ridiculed the staff and only attended group therapy because his barrister for his up and coming trial had said that it would help his case.

The hospital had decreed that Telling had no mental illness, he was not dangerous. His main issue was that he was simply emotionally immature, and had never had enough love and affection in his life.

He was released from the hospital on Wednesday

21st April 1982, after nine weeks at St. Andrews. As the trial was a month away, Lou decided to stay in England for that.

A condition of Telling's bail was that he had to sign into High Wycombe police station daily, to prevent flight or absence without the authority of the police or court.

High Wycombe station was chosen for him. It was, after all, more convenient for him.

When the matter was scheduled for court, I attended. I had submitted my recommendation to my senior officers, to the prosecuting barrister and to the judge, as the matter was heard at Aylesbury Crown Court. Monika and Lou sat close to Telling.

His defence stated that he had shown maturity by entering St. Andrews voluntarily and dealing with his issued. He deeply regretted breaking the law, by ignorance rather than any criminal intent, and the matter was played down. I was never mentioned.

My recommendation was that Telling must receive a short sharp shock, you were allowed to make such recommendations in those days. A short spell in prison at the very least was essential, to stop any further stupidity happening, and to protect Monika Zumsteg-Telling at the very least. She had felt that her life was in danger, and I concurred.

My recommendation was totally ignored by all concerned. A substantial fine was imposed in court, but in a closed court session, unheard of in such a case before. This term is only applied to a trial that is held in private and is the opposite of an open court.

There are very few reasons for this, most include

an element of national security, and public and press are omitted. National security, not very minor members of the aristocracy who appear to have committed a minor indiscretion!

Telling pleaded guilty to each of the charges, and when sentence was passed, Telling's only comment was to ask if he could write the court a cheque, a cheque that was obviously to be drawn on the Vestey Trust bank account. No real punishment, no reason not to reoffend. The case was over in minutes, but the repercussions would never be over. The man who had spent two months in private mental institutions seemed miraculously healed. Under normal circumstances, I, as the arresting officer would have read his antecedents to the court before sentence. On this occasion I was not required to do so, and I received no mention. This had been anything but normal after all.

Outside the court, the grinning Telling was heard to say, "In this country you can get away with anything if you have the money to do so". I considered reporting this, but really – what would have been the point.

This was not my last meeting with Michael Telling, and I only spoke to Monika once more, me having telephoned her to see if she was ok. She had said that she was unhappy and disappointed in the court result, but she was ok. She wanted to return to America, but she was trying to make things work for Michael. Hopefully it would all work out in the end. Maybe they could both go to America. I doubted it with his recent convictions, doubted that he would be allowed into the country, but as it turned out I was naive in that respect. Perhaps I should have realised that Telling had the backing and resources to go anywhere he wished, and indeed he would do so, as will be seen.

Vestey family barrister Michael Mansfield, in his own inimitable manipulative way had worked his magic, and not for the last time.

I saw Telling walk out of the Court in Aylesbury, grinning like a Cheshire cat as he walked down the steps in the Market Square. A Cheshire cat that had evaded justice, and indeed, not for the last time. At no time was the fact that he had held guns to Monika's head on more than one occasion mentioned in Court. None of the violence was mentioned either. It seems that it had either been glossed over, forgotten, or the statement that I had taken from the frightened lady had been lost, it had vanished. Michael Telling was just misunderstood, a little immature, that was all.

There was every intention on my part to do the right thing to follow things up, a welfare check occasionally. I had fully intended to check up on Monika again, but other work got in the way, and this to my everlasting regret.

One wonders what I would have found if I had attended Lambourne House after this travesty. As a police officer there are some smells that you can instantly identify, some smells you never forget.

Death is one such smell.

CHAPTER
TWENTY-ONE

I HAD HEARD through a friend that the weapons that I confiscated were being used in firearms training sessions.

I was aware that these particular weapons had never been found within the Thames Valley before. I was told that the power of the AR15 was tested in a controlled experiment in Milton Keynes. The gun was shot into a building estate. The velocity took the bullet through two houses, I was informed. The training session where the weapons were produced, I was given to understand, was grossly exaggerated. It was to become a lesson in how NOT to disarm a man with a gun. How not to. I wonder what the correct way is when your life is in jeopardy? As a result, I handed in my permit to carry a firearm whilst on duty.

The next time I came into contact with Michael Telling was in Thame, Oxfordshire. I, and other police officers would utilise a public house called 'The Birdcage', a pub with a history dating back to the year

1300. It was a watering hole, and a place to unwind in peace.

It was a couple of months after the Crown Court case. As I walked up to the pub, I noticed a Harley-Davidson motor cycle parked outside. This was unusual in itself, but the machine was the California Highway Patrol livery version. I had only ever seen one other in the UK before, but a sticker on the rear panier was not police issue. It read '***SOCIETY FUCKS***'.

My keen police trained mind soon put two and two together and came up with four. I had only ever seen such machines in California, and in a garage in Radnage, at Lambourne House. I walked into the bar, and there stood at the bar, was a comical figure, dressed from head to toe in a C.H.I.P.S uniform complete with helmet.

"Hello Mister Thrift" he said. It was Michael Telling. He had clearly found out our watering hole and decided to join the party.

I admit to loosing my temper. *I was furious that he had the bloody cheek to think that he could waltz into my life again.* The cowardly liar was the last person in the world that I wanted to see. My suggestion was that he left the pub immediately, and never returned. I suggested that it would be in his own interest, and he did so. He had ruined my day anyway. I heard the screech of tyres as he left Thame. My dislike for Telling had surfaced again, and not for the last time.

That was the last time that I ever saw Michael Telling, but not the last time that he would enter my life.

Maybe I was cursed in that respect.

CHAPTER
TWENTY-TWO

LIFE CONTINUED, as it does, and I was transferred to High Wycombe C.I.D. It was a very busy posting.

A caste murder, a man intent on shooting a love rival and other matters happened rapidly, and all needed complete concentration.

I did not forget Michael Telling or Monika, who would forget them, but circumstances prevailed, other crime happened, and life went on. Nothing more came to light about Michael Telling for some time. One presumed that he had changed his ways, had learnt his lesson and would not reoffend, but the truth was very far from that.

In reality, little had changed. His court case was over, money assured that. But it made not one iota of difference to the little boy who never grew up. No not Peter Pan, but Michael Telling.

Things continued as they had before, and he continued to invite his biker 'friends' to Lambourne

House, and drank to excess with them, even in the presence of his father in-law, Lou. Obviously, Michael provided the drink. Shaven heads, and those with hair had it dyed all shades of the rainbow. Lou Zumsteg was shocked to see them at the house, and even more shocked at Michael Telling's boasts of his wealth. The 'friends' were clearly impressed with his Harley-Davidsons, especially the C.H.I.P.S. model and his sheriff uniform. But these were not enough for Telling. He boasted that he could afford any motorcycle in the world, in fact he was so rich, there was nothing out of reach to him – he could afford anything he wanted, forever. It impressed the gathering, but not Lou or his daughter Monika. These fair-weather friends sometimes remarked on his watches, and just like the time in America, like the Arab royalty, Telling would give then the watch. It was only money, after all. And it was, like buying a pub full of people drinks, the way that Michael Telling purchased his 'friends'.

Lou persuaded Telling to take more responsibility for his own actions, to actually earn his keep. To get a job, and actually find some real friends who were not just after his wealth, to get whatever they wanted from pretence. The two decided on an Import - export business. Importation from and export to America. British bikes and accessories one-way, American bikes and accessories the other way. Perfect for two lovers of motor-cycles.

And so, Lou Zumsteg returned to California a happy man. He had seen the end to Michael's bad ways, he thought, the court case was behind him. He had talked him into being more responsible, and being responsible for his own actions. Taking care of his diabetes and controlling his moods by doing so. Telling had agreed to start a business, a joint venture, and Monika's had agreed to at least try to be more understanding of her husband, more supportive and less critical. The business would do him good. Would occupy his mind on things other than CB radio and hangers on.

I had seemed the idea situation. The situation to end a bad chapter in Michael's life, a very bad chapter. Things could only get better, couldn't they? Everyone was happy and smiley now. But how long could it last? Exactly how long could Telling stay enthusiastic about anything that was not just handed to him on a sterling silver spoon?

Only time would tell. Only Telling could tell.

CHAPTER
TWENTY-THREE

LIFE WENT ON IN BUCKINGHAMSHIRE, for me and for Monika and Michael.

The winter of early 1982 in the United Kingdom, also called The Big Snow of 1982 by the press, was a severe cold wave that was formed in early December 1981 and lasted until early in 1982, and was one of the coldest Decembers recorded in the United Kingdom. The lowest recorded temperature was: −27.2 degrees C. Later that year the temperature rose to just under 30 degrees C. Unusual weather even for England.

In the year that a British task force successfully liberated the Falkland Islands after they were captured by Argentinians, Spain joined NATO, Helmut Kohl replaced Helmut Schmidt as chancellor of West Germany, and Yuri Andropov took over as leader of the Soviet Union. In the music world, 'Thriller' by Michael Jackson was released and the chart-topper of the year in the UK was 'Come on Eileen' by Dexy's Midnight Runners.

Monika Zumsteg-Telling took several temp jobs whilst awaiting the outcome of her application to Oxford, a start date. Unlike most temps, she sometimes arrived at work in a chauffeur driven car. After Oxford, she had decided that she wished to pursue a career in law, eventually elevating herself to barrister. Perhaps her experience at Aylesbury Crown Court had changed her mind, but whatever it was, she decided against a career in computing.

Outwardly the couple seemed happy. Monika was off the drink and happy to sip Coke instead.

Meanwhile, relations with the Vestey trust were growing ever thinner. It is known that every expense had to be authorised by Mr Brown and the trust. The horse that Monika had so desired was not forthcoming, and she located another and requested it from the trust. She was told that someone from the trust would secure the sale. Nothing happened until weeks later she found out that no such representation had been made, and the beautiful chestnut had been sold to someone else.

It appeared that she was under pressure keep Michael on the straight and narrow path, to assure no further embarrassment to the Vestey name, and to kerb his excessive expenses, and to soft soap her husband. Vestey family business was private, whatever it was, and not for public consumption – ever.

Within weeks things changed, as they were always bound to do. Michael Telling never did have a great span of attention of enthusiasm for things other than spending money, expensive fast cars, Harley-Davidsons, football, and boys toys, expensive boys toys. He had stopped seeing his expensive psychiatrist, stopped looking for work – if he ever started – and all thoughts of the import/export business and garage in High Wycombe were abandoned, like Monika's dreams.

Oxford had gone back on their previous decision that her excellent work record in the States was sufficient, and now said that she was required to take an entrance test. One wonders what or who influenced this decision. She was never told the subject of the test, never given any opportunity to study for it.

English history and the history of politics in England were subjects that the California girl knew little of. But they were the chosen subjects, chosen by someone to embarrass Monika perhaps. She was encouraged to re sit the entrance exam, but it was all too little, too late. The girl who hated failure in anything failed. She had failed to get into Oxford, and despite her efforts her marriage was failing.

What could she do, where could she go now to make herself feel in any way a useful member of society?

CHAPTER
TWENTY-FOUR

THE INADEQUATE BOY who grew up to be the inadequate man was obsessed with citizens band radio, CB. 'Chief Inspector' ruled the airwaves in the High Wycombe area, with tales of fantasy, tales of daring- do, adventures of a hero.

Adventures of a special forces soldier and spy. A very special man with unlimited money. Easy pray for any gold digger in the area.

Easy pray for young women that he spoke to late into the night. The Don Juan, lecher, lounge lizard conveniently forgot his new wife in another room nearby as he spouted his rhetoric to the nearby gold-diggers, eager to meet the local hero.

He would disappear at all hours to meet these fans. He had been married to Monika for less than a year, but he always wanted more. He was very generous with gifts, particularly as they were always charged to a card and paid through the trust. Monika noticed several charges for flowers and other things. She questioned Michael Telling, who lied that they were for relatives, friends, special occasions. Nothing for her to worry about.

But something perhaps for him to worry about, as after that she would never get to the post first, never see the bills. I believe that Monika thought that a child would be the cure of all ills, to indeed tame the beast that Michael Telling, and as her admission to Oxford was no longer a stopping point, and the fact that wanted a child immediately, Monika agreed.

She fell pregnant quickly, but lost the baby after a short while, painfully for her both mentally and physically. Instead of sympathy, Telling was furious. He made it very clear that he blamed her, stormed out and went to Torquay to see his son Matthew for the next week.

He returned home to Monika's forgiveness. He gave her a blue fox fur coat to make up for his overreaction. In the next month, the couple visited Edinburgh and Morocco, where they had been before, but Monika remained unhappy. Telling had at least admitted to being a habitual liar, and Monika believed that by staying with Michael, she would feed his addiction to lies, and that in doing so, he would never recover.

Shortly after her return, she telephoned America, said she wanted to return home for Christmas, without Michael. Her mother talked her out of that, saying how hard it would be for them to be separated at Christmas. It would be good for her, for them. Monika concurred, and they both went to Santa Rosa for Christmas.

Michael went to San Francisco to visit acquaintances at the Dudley Perkins agency, and to meet members of the family. It is the third-oldest motorcycle dealership in the United States. It has been run by the same family for that entire time, with the third generation of the Perkins' involved in the business at this time.

Dudley Perkins settled in San Francisco in 1912. At the time, the city was a bustling waterfront town, largely recovered from the 1906 earthquake and fire. Motorcycles were popular — in 1911, the San Francisco Motorcycle Club boasted 500 members, including the mayor! Dudley started his San Francisco Harley-Davidson agency in 1914 with a partner, who he bought out in 1917. He was an avid racer who later became a champion hillclimber, and his race winnings sometimes kept the business going in tough times.

Dudley also had innovative ideas, including starting a fleet of commercial sidecars for rent. Businesses that offered deliveries to customers could rent a package truck outfit, which would be stored and serviced at the dealership as part of the deal. Dudley would even locate a driver for the outfit.

They were motorcycle royalty to Michael Telling. Meanwhile Monika and her mother shopped until they dropped for the next few days, and then they both travelled to Reno, to the casinos, but a sandstorm prevented their arrival.

Eight miles outside Reno is the Boomtown Casino and hotel. Elsa won big time, but Monika clearly had her mind on other things. Elsa liked Michael, but as Monika explained, she only knew one side of him. She had not seen the childish sulking, nor the violent tempers. Monika said that although she really did love him, and that he had, once again, agreed to see his psychologist, seek gainful employment, and try to live an independent life of the Vestey's and the Vestey trust. Talk is indeed cheap, and Telling was full of that. They say he was charming, but I certainly never saw one iota of charm, but it appears that Monika's parents found him that way. Monika agreed that she could never stay angry with him for long, no matter what he did, however bad it was.

She agreed to give him one more chance, he was at least worth that. But if it did not work, she was coming back to America, to California, and return to computing.

Elsa agreed that Monika could achieve anything that she put her mind too. Christmas was pleasant, and the visit was considered a success by all concerned. How fickle life is, and how quickly things can change. A leopard cannot change its spots.

Neither could Michael Telling change his personality, nor actually promise something, mean it and stick to it.

CHAPTER
TWENTY-FIVE

ON RETURN TO ENGLAND, it has been said that Monika was taking less care of her appearance.

One has to wonder if that was true. She wore less makeup, and wore spectacles more frequently. She also lost a considerable amount of weight in a short time. She suffered from severe migraine, and things at Lambourne were not improving.

Unsurprisingly, Michael Telling had not stuck to any of his promises. No job, no psychiatrist, complete refusal to take any responsibility for anything, and the childish temper tantrums continued as before. He had again smashed up the house in a rage. Monika was becoming desperate to leave, but had nowhere to go, and no funds to do it with.

I have been told that Monika had managed to squirrel some money away, if she ever did need to make a quick exit. But in one of his destructive rages, he found the box containing it and set fire to the money, stating that she would never, ever leave him.

Monika's mother suggested that she speak to Mr Brown, and move to an apartment in London, but Monika knew, or feared that Mr Brown would tell Telling of her whereabouts. Monika said that if she was able to leave, she would slip away and leave everything she had at Lambourne.

The now unhappy couple became even more unhappy, but much worse was to come.

Within three months of the new year, and less than a year since his court case Telling had still not sought medical help, and Monika delivered an ultimatum. Get help, or I am leaving. He went into another rant, Telling reacted, over reacted. He booked himself into St Andrews again, called Dimmick, and stated that he wanted a divorce, but did not tell Monika. In early March, he drove her to her temp job in High Wycombe, stating that he would pick her up later, and that they would have an evening out in Windsor.

Telling did not pick her up, but she eventually returned to Lambourne by taxi. The house had again been demolished from the inside out. Most of the furniture was missing, and the telephone line ripped out. She had been left with nothing but a note Even that had been written for him by Dimmick, his solicitor, days previously. It stated that he had gone, was not coming back, and that Mr Dimmick would inform her of what arrangements had been made for her financial support. It was the 11th March 1983.

Monika ran to a neighbour's house and telephoned America. She told her mother the situation, and what Telling had done this time and that she wanted to come home – she had had enough.

Elsa agreed that Monika had done her best to save the marriage, and now it was time to come home, and that she would wire her the money she needed.

Her father, Lou, said that she should get legal representation for herself, quickly. The Vestey clan would try every trick in every book written to win again. Vesteys did not like to fail, and rarely did. He also said that arrangements should be made to ship her belongings back to America, and Monika agreed.

Monika went to the home of two friends in Lane End, around a six minute drive. She used their telephone to call America again, then invited Cheryl Richardson to Lambourne to witness the destruction and devastation. Cheryl noticed that one thing undamaged was Michaels collection of vintage wines. The pair agreed to sample some of the most expensive in the collection, and so one of the wheels fell off and as a result, Monika fell right off the AA wagon.

One, two, three bottles or more were consumed. It was good stuff, but there were consequences.

The next day, with a hangover, Monika penned a reply to Telling's Farewell note. The private note was made public property, and a matter of public record when used at subsequent court proceedings to show her mental state! It read:

'Michael,

Thank you,

I am finally free

I sincerely hope that you find a cure for your illness as I found mine.

I will always keep the memories of Bermuda, and the

way I felt when I opened the door in L.A. and you were standing there, suitcase in hand.

Those were happy times. Maybe we should have stayed in L.A. England has never been good to either of us. Leave it as I intend to and never look back. Watch out for fair weather friends. Stand up for yourself. A.A. says 'We are not better, but no worse than the next person. I am leaving you the dishes and the things in the cabinets. Your mail is also there.

If you cannot find happiness, please go back to Al-Anon. You found help and friendship there.

Remember the cheese soup, Bermuda, and then we both can continue life with good memories of each other.

Goodbye and love always Monika'

Monika had been in England for seventeen months.

CHAPTER
TWENTY-SIX

DAVID STEWART WAS an agent for Oceanair International Movers Limited of Enfield, Middlesex. David remembers that her request was unusual.

In normal circumstances a representative would visit and give a detailed costing based on what he saw, what was to be moved, and to where.

But Monika just wanted a cost, based on her inventory. No one was to visit, she had said. She was an American, moving back to Santa Rosa following a failed marriage to in Englishman. She wanted to leave quietly, discreetly and without fuss. If a representative called, her husband may try to stop her, so any quotation had to be based on her inventory.

The company was known to her, and vice-versa, as they had been responsible for shipping her belongings from America seventeen months previously.

The list was short and succinct. It consisted of a few personal effects, a small amount of furniture, a parrot and a Pontiac Firebird car. The cost came to a total of £3000. The Vestey trust would pay that, she said, through the company representative, Mr Brown.

At the same time, Michael Telling was making his own preparations to leave. Gone was the resolve to attend the expensive hospital. Having dropped off Monika in High Wycombe that morning, 11th March, he had returned to Lambourne House and packed a few things. Oddly they included a television. Having stashed other items, including motorcycle parts in a summerhouse to which a sauna was being installed, he drove to his ex wife and left some of the items there.

He then went to his half-sisters home. She was the daughter of his mothers second husband. He stashed some items there and she drove him to Gatwick airport. He was going to Australia whilst the divorce was being sorted out. He would be taking a private helicopter flight to Heathrow. He had expected Monika to have called the police. He had probably broken his terms of probation, and had certainly not asked permission to leave the country.

But he was Michael Telling. His family did not need to do such things.

Monika had asked a friend to recommend a divorce lawyer, which they did. The lawyer was in London, and Monika attended an appointment. On arrival, on learning which family he would be up against in the divorce proceedings, he declined to take the case. He did not have either the stomach, guts nor skill to fight the Vestey family. A second solicitor was equally useless.

Telling's solicitors informed her where he, Telling

was, that he was in Australia, and that they were instructed to start divorce proceedings on his behalf. It was agreed that they would send her some living expenses, pay for the shipping of her possessions back to America, and to buy her a one-way ticket home. They were at pains to remind her of the pre-nup that she had previously signed.

Monika's parents were most anxious for her to return home to America, but she said that she wanted to conclude her dental surgery, due to be carried out at The Chiltern Hospital in Great Missenden, Buckinghamshire, a private hospital, within the next few days. She would be put under a general anaesthetic and unable to travel for a few days, but she intended to go to France or Italy before coming home.

Over the next couple of weeks, Monika's strong resolve faded. Headaches and depression followed, and if she left, she would surely miss some aspects of England at least. She would miss people from Tunbridge Wells and West Wycombe, the English pubs, and her little antique business. She would miss the welcoming pubs, and particularly miss her local, The Boot at Bledlow Ridge – just down the road from Lambourne House.

Monika was seen in The Boot, crying into a glass of orange juice.

She told someone who recognised her about her marital problems, the divorce, and the fact that she still loved Michael Telling. Foolish girl.

CHAPTER
TWENTY-SEVEN

'And once you are awake, you shall remain awake eternally.' ~**Friedrich Nietzsche**

SHORTLY AFTER THE BOOT SITUATION, Monika invited some friends from Tunbridge Wells to visit her for the last time at Lambourne House, before she returned to America for good.

She had the telephone line fixed, but forewarned them of the state of the place and what they should expect – devastation.

She had cleaned as best she could but it was a mere sticking plaster over a gaping wound. and the damage that he had caused was still obvious.

Over dinner she explained to her guests, the problems that she had, the moods and the rages, as if it was not obvious from the damage. She stated that whilst she wished to remain in England, she had decided to return to California and to resume her education, career and life there. She was determined to do just that.

But that determination changed and her resolve dissolved like the candles on the dinner table had burnt away. In the early hours of the morning the telephone rang. It was answered by David, her friend from Tunbridge Wells.

It was Michael Telling calling from Australia, demanding to speak to his wife. David said that Michael wanted to come back, to come home. The message was relayed from Monika that he could come back on condition that he resumes psychiatric help, and actually kept appointments.

Telling was furious at this and demanded to speak to Monika. And she made the mistake of speaking to him. She repeated what had already been said about getting help and sticking to it.

Unfortunately, Telling agreed with the condition of his return, and said that he would be on the next flight home.

There is some speculation that Monika spent the night with a Bledlow Ridge local, who had a thing for her, and who had previously been spurned by her.

What is known is that Telling called again from Singapore, and said he was en route home. Monika agreed to meet him in London and discuss any future that they may have.

They met at the beautiful Hyde Park Hotel in Knightsbridge., and talked. Monika had decided to be the one who would make the decisions, pull Telling's strings. Telling agreed and said he would go back to St. Andrews immediately, and that Monika should cancel her removals. They could work it out for sure, and Mr Brown was told to cancel the divorce.

Telling knew very well that Monika had vulnerabilities, like we all do. But Monika's was jewellery. Playing to this vulnerability, Telling had purchased a beautiful and expensive Cartier diamond necklace, paid for obviously once again by the Vestey trust.

The couple stayed the night at the Hyde Park Hotel, and the next day Telling recanted his previous promises. The couple argued and Monika called the chauffeur to get back to Lambourne House.

That was it. Monika had done her best but it had not worked. Finished.

Again, the resolve disappeared quickly. Michael called again and again promised that he would indeed attend St Andrews, and the next morning the couple drove to the facility. Clearly the previous therapy had failed, and it was decided he needed an extended stay of three months. Telling objected initially but later agreed, and it was decided that he would return in four days' time, once Monika's next bout of dental surgery at The Chilterns was completed.

Telling was seen acting strangely that weekend, whilst Monika was in The Chilterns Hospital, but asked for some help from a local in fitting something in his Mini Cooper.

Monika returned home two days later, and whilst still in discomfort, they needed to celebrate. To celebrate the surgery and to celebrate the reconciliation.

The venue for the celebration was to be Needham's snooker and bingo hall in Desborough Road, High Wycombe. Monika wore a T shirt with a camel cartoon figure on the front, and an expensive new Cartier diamond necklace.

The local was the designated driver, and later described them as an odd couple, always bickering but clearly in love. But more like a mother and child relationship.

That evening they returned to Lambourne, and Telling packed for his stay at St. Andrews Hospital. Telling had described the hospital as being more like a holiday camp than a nuthouse. Lots of trees and lawns and lovely women.

Monika had decided to take a trip whilst Michael was at St Andrews, maybe somewhere in Europe.

The local left at around midnight, saying that he would return in the morning to say goodbye to Michael before he went to St. Andrews.

The next morning, when he arrived at Lambourne House, just before midday, Telling was not dressed. He said he had changed his mind and would not be going to St. Andrews at all. He further stated that Monika had left for Europe for a brief holiday.

The local had seen the moods and the actions and reactions. He thought that they had more likely had another argument, and she had left again.

The truth was very far from that though. A week later, Telling drove to Devon again to see his ex-wife Alison and his son. He told her that he had returned from Australia in a last-ditch attempt to save his marriage, but it had not worked. He said that Monika had left, he knew not for where, nor did he care. He said that in any case she was only after his money.

And he said how much he appreciated Alison, and handed her a Cartier diamond necklace as a gift.

Telling purchased two German shepherd dogs and planted quick growing conifers around Lambourne House, effectively hiding him and Lambourne from locals and prying eyes.

A visitor the next week noted Monika's beloved Pontiac in the garage and asked Michael Telling if he had heard from her. Telling said that he had and that she had gone for good. In any event he would never take her back.

By then, Monika was dead. She had been shot several times with a high-powered hunting rifle, and her body was decomposing in the half built nearby sauna.

CHAPTER
TWENTY-EIGHT

HE HAD FINALLY SNAPPED.

Monika loved Michael Telling for all his very many faults. Even though he had threatened her with his boys toys, his guns before, she felt some sorrow for him when I took his guns that were later awarded to the Thames Valley Police. So much so that she purchased him another on a trip to America.

The laws of Australia meant that the purchase of a firearm, unlike in the United Kingdom was easy. An address on a driving licence was sufficient – and no police record meant that one just had to select a weapon of choice and pay for it.

Telling would have been unable to buy a weapon legally, anywhere else, and England was far stricter than any other country. His previous convictions excluded him in America on dozens of Californian penal codes.

The chosen weapon was the Winchester Marlin 336W underleaver rifle .30-30, a hunting rifle. One has to wonder how much hunting Telling could have done in Buckinghamshire, even if he could have legally possessed such a weapon. One has to wonder his intention on purchasing such a weapon. That particular rifle was made to hunt deer-sized and black bear-sized game. Not too many black bears in Bucks. The publicity on the weapon states that it unfortunately, the cartridge, with flat or round-nosed bullets, does not meet minimum energy standards required for moose hunting in Finland, Norway, or Sweden.

I sincerely believe that what happened next was very much premeditated as whilst in Australia, Telling had purchased the rifle and a quantity of soft nose ammunition, and had smuggled it back into the country, walking it through customs at Heathrow airport in his luggage. Once again, why would he have purchased the gun and the ammunition there and then if not for a specific purpose – to commit a murder.

What actually did happen on Tuesday 29th March 1983 is somewhat conjecture, as there is only one side of the story told, and that person was a proven liar. The other side, the side I tend to believe, is from the expert forensic reconstruction.

Home Office ballistic experts speculated that she was shot four times. Later the defence would even argue that he only shot her three times. Because that really mattered.

No doubt, Monika was furious that he had decided, despite his promises and her conditions for getting back together, that he would not attend St. Andrews the next day. No doubt there were angry words exchanged.

Telling already had the loaded weapon with him in the house. One wonders why. It has been said that the first shot was as she faced him. It hit her in the throat, and one can only imagine the size of the exit wound.

Exit wounds are usually larger than the entrance wound and this is because as the round moves through the body of the victim it slows down and explodes within the tissue and surrounding muscle.

As Monika sunk to her knees Telling ejected the spent cartridge, re cocked the gun and shot her again. He hit her in the chest.

He then ejected and reloaded again, twice – although the defence contention was that it was only once more, and the hollow point slugs made absolutely sure that Monika Elizabeth Zumsteg Telling was dead beyond a shadow of a doubt. It has been said that Telling checked for vital signs, just in case, but there were none. I very much doubt that, as with the amount of blood loss, and the damage caused, it would have been unnecessary to have done so, pointless.

A short time later, around the time that he was expected at St. Andrews hospital, Telling calmly telephoned the hospital and told them he would not be attending after all. It was, after all, Monika who had insisted on it.

And now Monika was dead and he did not have to do anything he didn't want to now.

CHAPTER
TWENTY-NINE

WHAT FOLLOWS NEXT IS a mixture of conjecture, the word of Telling, and fact.

I believe that his actions following the shooting were carefully thought out – not the actions of a man either grieving, sorry for his actions, regretful, remorseful, or penitent. They were the actions of a calculated man who had a plan. A plan to get away with murder.

He withdrew cash from an ATM machine using Monika's credit cards.

A few days later, he moved Monika's body to a camp bed in one of the bedrooms. It is said that he covered her body with a plastic motorcycle cover. Feeling deep regret for his actions he kissed her. Such regret that he left the body there for the next few weeks, pausing to either speak to her or kiss her as he passed by.

He then moved her body to the summerhouse and

to the partially built sauna, where she would remain for several months.

As time went by, Telling's confidence grew. He destroyed Monika's passport and her personal papers. He destroyed all signs of her. He returned to his old ways, and his enthusiasm for CB radio returned.

He even asked people to Lambourne, and asked women that had heard the rich lothario over the CB airways for sex, although it was said that on most occasions he was unable to perform.

To the outside world, life went on for Michael Telling, without Monika. When asked about her his answers were many and varied. She had gone back to America or had left him for another man, amongst other stories. And people believed him as he was, after all, a very practiced and believable liar.

He continued to make cashpoint withdrawals from her bank account, emptying her account, to prove to anyone interested that she was still alive.

He was becoming paranoid. People kept constantly asking about Monika, where was she, how was she. He suspected that he was being followed by someone, and that people were taking covert photographs of him, that his telephone was being tapped. He was becoming desperate. He told Monika's parents that she had left him, and burnt all correspondence for her. He continued to entertain 'friends' at Lambourne, and for five months – throughout one of the hottest summers in England – Monika's body remained in the sauna. He would go there and speak to her. He still loved her, after all.

Things were about to get even stranger, even more bizarre in this story.

CHAPTER
THIRTY

THE PARANOIA in Michael Telling grew exponentially.

Five months after the murder, he had to make a decision, what to do next. He had got away with it before, he would get away with it again. Absolutely no need to panic, not yet anyway.

Lambourne house was due to have its annual sprucing, painting and decorating, and it would happen sometime in September. If he did not ack quickly, the game would be well and truly up. They would find Monika's body – the smell would assure that.

And so Michael Telling would have to take some drastic action. He would have to move the woman he loved to another location, somewhere far away where she would not be found, and identified, and she could not be connected to Michael Telling.

Was this the mind of a mentally ill man? Or was it the mind of a calculated man, running scared, once again attempting to run away from what he had done and once again failing to stand up to the very serious consequences of his actions.

But in the worst case scenario, if ever caught, if ever convicted he would go to prison. In England, the punishment for murder is fixed by law. There was only one punishment for murder, life imprisonment.

The last executions in the United Kingdom were by hanging, and took place in 1964, prior to capital punishment being suspended for murder in 1965 and finally abolished in 1969. Had the murder been committed in California, and had he been convicted, the result would have been somewhat different.

Capital punishment, execution by lethal injection is a legal penalty in the U.S. state of California. The state carried out 720 executions from 1778 to the 1983. If only.

But it was not to be. He had escaped prison before, and he was determined to do it once more. He hired a van from a hire agency in nearby West Wycombe Road, High Wycombe, on 1st September, and asked a local for a lift there to collect it. He had said he had a large amount of rubbish to take to the council dump.

But that was not where he was headed. He had loaded several items into the van by nightfall. They included one of the dogs, a fishing rod and bait, a tent, a spade and an axe. If nothing was pre decided, if Michael Telling was mentally ill, then why would he need an axe to bury a body?

The drive took some time, the weather was bad. Michael Telling drove to a woods, just south of Exeter in Devon, just 22 miles from his ex wife and son. It was an area that he knew well.

Reports of what happen differ here. What is totally clear is that Michael Telling was going to bury Monika's body in the woods outside Exeter. He dug a shallow grave and put her body into it. He said he loved her so much that he could not bear to leave her there. So very quickly he decided to take her back home, or part of her anyway. Completely without forethought, he took out the otherwise useless axe from the van and chopped off her head.

He then drove back to Lambourne house with the head of his wife in the rented van.

CHAPTER
THIRTY-ONE

TELLING DROVE BACK to Lambourne House.

The previous evening he had telephoned a local to ask them to feed the young Alsatian puppy that he had left at Lambourne, whilst he was away on a mission. When the local arrived to feed the dog the next morning, he was surprised to see Telling and both dogs there. It was apparent that Telling had hosed out the hired van, which was also there and near to one of the garages - how odd.

The next day he did visit the local council rubbish tip, and took with him some items for a neighbour and some plastic rubbish bags. He did not say what they contained. He was accompanied in this mission by neighbour Richard Richardson, who later, once again helped him clean and wash out the van before it was returned to the hire depot.

Sometime later, Telling asked Richard's wife to accompany him to a supermarket to buy supplies. He had invited his first wife Alison, and his son to Lambourne. Richard's wife innocently asked after Monika, and Telling said that she was dead and that he had killed her. The story seemed fantastical, and she did not believe him, and Telling said no more.

When they returned to Lambourne, Telling invited them and their two sons to join him there for dinner, to which they agreed.

Whilst awaiting the food, a television was playing in Lambourne House. The news came on and there was the shocking news that a headless female corpse had been found in woods near Exeter. Telling excused himself, and was then heard to vomit. They all put it down to a hypo from Telling's diabetes, something that they had witnessed before, and that he had always failed to deal with correctly. No more was mentioned about it.

The next day, Alison and Telling's son Matthew arrived from Torquay, and the Richardson's arrived with their sons, for the children to play together at Lambourne House.

Telling was giving the summer house, the soon to be, and currently part built sauna room, an airing he explained. He said that it was getting stuffy in there. There were some stains on the floor, and boxes of Monika's things, that they had helped pack up months before and they thought had been shipped to her.

Telling said he had been too busy to get around to sending them on, but would do so, soon. He had more important things to do. He was more interested to know if they thought there was an odour in there.

This despite the presence of the air purifier that Monika had purchased him the previous February 14th, and for which she received a black eye.

CHAPTER
THIRTY-TWO

THERE HAVE BEEN several conflicting stories about exactly what happened next. I will tell the version used in court, and the other one that I was told.

When I saw a subsequent news bulletin, I had been out of the country at the time of the initial discovery of the body. The police had a good idea as to the identity of the body in Exeter. at the same time that it was seen by Christina, it appears that we both recognised the T shirt that the corpse was found dressed in. The label said that it was made in Thailand, but we both suspected that it had been purchased in Morocco. The reason for contacting me was very simple. I had been the only police officer that knew him, had interviewed him several times and arrested him. No more than that. By the time I made the call, officers were already at the scene, and a discovery had been made.

I was told that Monika's head was put into the freezer in one of the garages at Lambourne House by

Telling. Wrapped in several bin liners, Telling would take it out of the freezer, unwrap the head and talk to her and kiss her occasionally. It was described to me as a bizarre kind of pass the parcel.

The second version was that after Telling was detained, Devon and Cornwall Scenes of Crime, the UK equivalent of the US CSI, found a black plastic bag on the parcel shelf of his Mini Cooper in the same garage. It contained multiple bags again. On unwrapping them, the officers were confronted with a human head.

In both versions, the sight that greeted them was upsetting, even to the most hardened, hairy arsed copper. A dead body, or part of one, has a rank and pungent smell mixed with a tinge of sickening sweetness. Imagine a rotting piece of meat with a couple drops of cheap perfume and you're halfway to understanding what a human corpse, or part of one smells exactly like. The smell that any policeman can smell from a distance. The smell that would have been so obvious if it had been smelt in the back of a Mini Cooper.

The skin was rotting and putrefied. It actually turns like a sea blue-green colour. Most of her teeth, so carefully righted at The Chilterns Hospital were missing.

This caused a problem. One part of the body was in Devon and Cornwall, the other part in the Thames Valley coroners areas. After consultation, it was decided that Devon and Cornwall had won the case, and the head was to be reunited with her body and taken to Exeter. Michael Henry Maxwell Telling was briefly questioned, and he admitted to having killed Monika. He was arrested, and like some of the mortal remains of her wife, he was transported to Exeter,

Back at Lambourne House, Scenes of Crime did their work. Whatever happened in court, they would have to prove beyond a reasonable doubt, exactly what had happened here.

It is a matter of public record that a neighbour, close to Monika was beyond upset.

She knew of Telling's recent court case at Aylesbury, and remarked, 'I wonder if the Vestey's will get him off of this one as well?' It was a certainty that they would try to, and that Michael telling would receive the best excuses in court that money could buy. Excuses and accusations aplenty.

After all, it could not be Michael Telling's fault could it. Michael Telling was a Vestey, and Vestey's were faultless. Weren't they?

CHAPTER
THIRTY-THREE

THE FAULTLESS MICHAEL TELLING had been arrested on suspicion of murder.

He had admitted to killing Monika, and was co-operating with the detectives from Devon and Cornwall, answering their questions. He said that he had shot her with the Marlin 30-30 rifle purchased in Australia. He no longer had the weapon. In his clear up, his attempt to get away with murder, he had broken down the weapon, and taken some parts to the council tip at Beaconsfield in the hired van, and other parts he had scattered along the verges of the M40 motorway.

He seemed more concerned about the welfare of his dogs than the position that he was in, and quickly told the detective in charge that Monika's head was in the garage. He explained that he could not leave the head with the body, that she would have been easily identified. He also said that he loved her too much and would occasionally talk to the head. He had not considered the clothing might identify her, as it had indeed done, and led to this moment.

And then the murderer showed his true colours. She had pushed him with her nagging. It was her fault, obviously. He could never take responsibility for his actions as a boy, or would he before as a man. Why should he start now?

He asked for his solicitor, Kenneth Dimmock, and decided to say no more until he had taken Dimmock's council. Probably sensible, but by then he had already admitted to killing Monika and to cutting her head off with the axe.

Having been taken to High Wycombe police station, and having met with Dimmock, his solicitor, Telling made a statement under caution, an admission to killing Monika. He also made many allegations against her.

Allegations that it would be impossible to disprove. Outrageous allegations that once said could never be unsaid. Once said they would leave a lasting impression on all that heard them, and cause a mini media frenzy.

I believe that Telling was many things, but one beyond any doubt is that he was a coward. A man that could never take responsibility for his own actions, he never would. Nothing was ever his fault. Naturally the main reason was that Monika was only after his money. This despite the pre-nup that Mr Brown and the Vestey clan had insisted on to prevent her receiving anything should the marriage fail. Many more accusations followed. She was lesbian, then she was bi sexual. She was an alcoholic, a user of marijuana, cocaine and heroin. She constantly belittled him, and laughed at his inadequacy sexually. The character assassination had started.

On the day of the murder, it was her fault. She kept telling him to hurry up and get ready to go to St. Andrews hospital, and taunting him. He picked up the rifle, and Monika shouted at him. She ran towards him, and he thought she might attack him and so he shot her. He just happened to have a loaded hunting rifle handy to prevent any verbal of physical attack that may happen, just in case. He really loved Monika, and if she had not constantly nagged at him, he would not have killed her, but he did and it was her fault after all.

Telling was then transported to Exeter police headquarters in Middlemore, Exeter.

It was necessary for Monika's head to be confirmed as belonging to the body that had been found, and at the same time that the teeth found with the body were the teeth from Monika's head. Obviously, it all fitted. The teeth had probably been knocked out with the violent decapitation.

Telling was charged with Monika's murder and put before the magistrates at Central Devon Magistrates court to be remanded in custody awaiting trial for murder. It was really a matter of course, and a taste of what was to come probably for the next twenty years at least.

He was transferred to the Category B Exeter prison to await trial. These are high security prisons, that house male prisoners who, if they were to escape, pose the most threat to the public, the police or national security. He was categorised as non employed rather than unemployed. The difference was that Michael Telling did not have to work.

It was necessary for the prosecution to determine the state of mind that Michael Telling had when he killed Monika. The main question was, was the killing premeditated. Detective Inspector Rundle from The Devon and Cornwall police, the man who had arrested and interviewed Telling believed so. He had formed the opinion during the car journey from high Wycombe to Exeter. He was convinced that his trip to Australia was all part of a plan, a premeditated plan to murder Monika. Mr. Rundle was equally convinced that George Carmen and the Vestey defence team would attempt to prove that it was simply a non-premeditated irrational act that he was pushed into. As such it would not be possible to prove the charge of murder – there was no malice aforethought.

John Hamilton was the last and youngest medical director of Broadmoor hospital, the prison for the criminally insane, and a leading forensic psychiatrist. At the age of 39 he went to one of the most onerous and responsible posts in psychiatry at a difficult time, facing problems of reorganisation and of the new Mental Health Act of Parliament, and an increased scrutiny of working practices. As medical director, he was responsible for many issues, including management of the hospital, a large staff, estate and budget, and for critical decisions about patients with complex mental disturbances who were dangerous or violent. At this time such patients included Ronnie Kray, Peter Sutcliffe, John Straffen, the longest-serving prisoner in

British history after he was sent to Broadmoor, after killing two girls in 1951, Ian Ball and Kenneth Erskine, the Stockwell Strangler. He was also tasked by the Director of Public Prosecutions, Major Sir Thomas Hetherington, to interview the prisoner on remand for another murder, a man named Michael Telling.

It is a matter of public record that on meeting, Telling talked constantly for two hours. His complaints about his treatment were first. The prison was overcrowded, his guards were unpleasant, the food was bad. He complained about the police, about Brian Rundle and Jeff Henthorne – his arresting officers. He complained about, and blamed Monika. It was her fault. At no time did he show any remorse, offer any contrition for killing her. Telling admitted to paying or treating fellow prisoners to gain favour, to pay for friendship. He also admitted to planning to kill Monika, and plotting how to carry it out. He had made the final decision to kill her the night before the murder by shooting her with the ammunition purchased specifically for that purpose. But Monika deserved to die, after all.

The fact that he had thought about it, and planned it in advance proved pre-meditation, malice aforethought beyond a doubt. The DPP agreed that it was definitely a case of murder, not manslaughter.

What was also definite was that with his reputation, whatever the truth was, George Carmen would not present it that way. It would not be Telling's fault, nothing ever was. He would surely present evidence to rebut anything that John Hamilton may say, anything that anyone would say against his client.

George Carmen would do anything to prove that Michael Telling was not of sound mind when he shot and killed Monika Zumsteg, and indeed he did just that, by assassinating, shooting down in flames, each and every prosecution witness.

CHAPTER
THIRTY-FOUR

PLEASE REMEMBER the words that a grinning Michael Telling had spoken as he walked down the steps from Aylesbury Crown Court.

He had said, "In this country you can get away with anything if you have the money to do so". How true that would prove to be.

Whilst Telling was remanded in custody, the officers of the Devon and Cornwall were completing the paperwork for submission to the Director of Public Prosecutions before court proceedings, before any trial, but the decision had been made on the murder charge.

It did not take long for the British newspapers to learn of the prisoner languishing in Exeter prison. The rich and influential prisoner and member of the rich and powerful Vestey family. Probably because his treatment and background was like no other before or since.

A man who was in prison with Telling anonymously wrote, "I was in Exeter prison with telling 1983 while he was on remand and he would sit and cry when he was questioned about her but he cried like a kid who was in trouble and wanted his mum... he certainly wasn't right mentally. I used to collect his lunch from the gate and he received a five star menu from an outside caterer... much of which he would give away to people (me included) as a way of keeping friends. Oysters, wine every meal as it was allowed on remand at that time..."

He also had carpet and a colour television in his cell. Someone had smuggled out photographs of his suffering there, and sent them to the News of The World, a now defunct Sunday red top newspaper, a scandal rag. It belonged to Rupert Murdock and was forced to close its pages due to a phone hacking scandal in 2011. They printed the scandalous story of the rich kid living a life of luxury in prison.

Somehow, they, the press, got to know of Telling's previous convictions just a short time before. One can only surmise that he may have told the photographer or another lag about his daring exploits. As a result, for some unknown reason, for several days at work at High Wycombe CID, I was followed every time I left the police station, and I was aware that I was being photographed. I still have no real idea why. However, I received calls from the News of The World and other red tops, asking for comments on Michael Telling. I referred these calls to the Thames Valley Police press office, as was dictated then, and received a call back saying, "You will not speak to the gutter press, under any circumstances".

Naturally I ignored that, and when approached in person by a reporter from the gutter press, my curiosity got the better of me and I agreed to a meeting in a pub away from High Wycombe later that evening. When I attended, the reported was obnoxious, *demanding* that I answer his ridiculous questions. I answered nothing, and had no intention of spilling any proverbial beans anyway. Who the hell did he think he was, demanding anything from me? I then finished my drink and left, but not before accidentally knocking his drink over and into his lap. I never heard anything more from the press on the matter, and neither was my meeting reported on.

The press was not slow in coming forward in Santa Rosa either. They made the lives of the Zumsteg family a misery. Skulking around, trying to photograph the grieving family from everywhere possible. They received calls from the British press for a comment.

A comment on the man who killed their daughter, the man who had changed their very private lives forever, and would forever do so, and go on to ruin more than one more life.

CHAPTER
THIRTY-FIVE

I WAS NOT INVOLVED in Telling's murder trial, nor was I ever again asked for an opinion, nor contacted by Devon and Cornwall about my previous dealings with him.

There was no reason, after all. But I did follow the trial with great interest, and an element of surprise. The trial and proceedings were not held 'in camera', and the proceeding are a matter of public record.

The newspapers in England had a field day with their lurid headlines. 'BIZARRE SEX LIFE OF RICH WIFE' reported The Sun. Monika was reported as 'AN ALCOHOLIC BISEXUAL WHO TOOK DRUGS'. 'TAUNTED HIM ABOUT HIS INADEQUATE LOVE-MAKING AND FLAUNTED HER LESBIAN AFFAIRS'. And about his subsequent conquests, 'LOVE SCENE AS WIFE LAY DEAD'. About his family, 'NEW SCANDAL ROCKS VESTEY EMPIRE'. The Vestey's only comment was that he was not a close member of the family. There was pretrial speculation, 'SOCIETY WIFE'S BODY KEPT IN FREEZER'. It was not the end of the press speculation. According to the vicious press, Monika was variously a 'PARTY GIRL' she held orgies at Lambourne house, she was a good time girl who mixed with the rich and famous, from rock stars to royalty.

Some aspects of trials in England cannot be reported on, or speculated on. The court, as previously in Aylesbury can censor them, gag them, but such rules do not apply to the dead. The dead have no rights, and both the press and the defendant can say anything they wish about them, however outrageous with immunity. One can only speculate on the feelings of Monika's grieving family, when the relentless assault on their privacy continued across the Atlantic, mercilessly. A few years later, these unfeeling animals would be responsible for another death, the death of a princess. When one thought it could not get any worse, that the press could not get any more vicious, it certainly would.

People started to come out of the woodwork, all manner of people, some that had never even met them, others who wished to remain anonymous. The next statement may be contentious, but it is true. My experience is that people will say anything for money, even purge themselves if the money is right. There are those who will say anything for publicity. Anything for their fifteen minutes of fame, to see their name in newsprint. No matter how outrageous the dead are painted. I have no evidence but I have my suspicions. How easy it is to allege anything about someone who cannot answer for themselves, cannot answer because you killed them. So easy to blacken someone's character and reputation. To this day I stick to my beliefs and to the belief of those people who were closest to her.

But a rich man from an infamous titled family was on trial for murder, not an everyday occurrence. And the unusual and sensational makes good copy and sells newspapers. The English love a bit of scandal, particularly involving the rich or famous, and this was a lot more than just a bit of scandal. Michael Telling made sure of that. A little more scandal every day, just enough to keep the press and public interested, and to make people feel sorry for the downtrodden Michael Telling, and it worked.

Meanwhile, all attempts to contact any member of the Vesteys by Monika's family failed. They had simply brushed Monika aside, and never expressed any condolence to her family. Requests for assistance in the repatriation of her body and property went unanswered, and eventually the family were informed that no member of the Vestey family would have direct contact, and nor would they assist them.

Indeed, British law gave Michael Telling all rights to Monika's property, unless he was found guilty of either her murder or her manslaughter.

Additionally, there was no money in her Lloyds bank account – Telling had emptied it after all, and her family had no reason to visit Lambourne House. It was sealed, all property removed and in storage, and after all, the property belonged to the Vestey trust, and Monika's father had no reason to visit there. Should he choose to come to England, he could collect her personal belongings from storage. They were against any service of remembrance in High Wycombe, and they suggested that Monika's acquaintances were not of 'the type' to attend anyway. In any event, any such service would be bound to attract even more publicity.

The car that Monika owned would have to be sold, and any monies raised would have to offset the ever-increasing storage costs now being paid by the trust. If Ella chose to accompany her husband in such an upsetting assignment, under no circumstances would the trust pay any of her expenses.

The difference between murder and manslaughter in law is vast, and the onus on proof is vast. Manslaughter is a less serious offence than murder. Although the result is the same in that the person has died, the main difference is in the intent of the attacker. Manslaughter is when a person kills another, but only intended to hurt them, or to exert some force on them.

Murder is defined in law as, when a person of sound mind unlawfully kills another person, with the intention to kill or cause grievous bodily harm.

The crime of murder carries a mandatory life sentence, if convicted. Sentence is fixed by law. Manslaughter, however, depending on the '*severity*' of the offence – and if it is classified as a voluntary or involuntary act – the maximum sentence for manslaughter in the UK is life imprisonment. However, the judge may impose a lesser sentence, including: A prison sentence – typically ranging between 2 and 10 years. I have never understood the meaning of the '*severity*'. Surely the result is the same, you have taken someone's life. But the law sees it differently.

Dimmock had a say in whom should defend Telling at his trial, and the choice was an easy one. Queens Council George Carmen was chosen. Who else. Personal experience of the man was that he was very good at his job, but his methods were questionable in my opinion. He was known to attack the credibility of witness against his client, and to belittle them or play down any importance that they may have. A police officer was used to such actions rather like an actor expecting the next lines, but civilians – the majority of whom had never set foot inside a court before, particularly with the pomp of a high court and a murder trial, the judge looking resplendent in his red robes, could never, ever have imagined the intrusive, some would say rude and dismissal mental assault that George Carmen would put them through.

One would wonder who was on trial, Telling or the witness. "What is it you do for a living? Oh is that all? How could you possibly think that a person like you, with a job like that could assist this court in any way?"

This would be the usual way that George Carmen would address a witness for the defence, and in this case in his defence of the admitted killer named Michael Telling.

CHAPTER
THIRTY-SIX

ATTACKING the credibility of a witness and their lifestyle, or the life or supposed lifestyle of a victim is a usual form of defence for a defendant and their council in a court of law.

Wrong or right that is the way it is in England and America. Immoral or ethical, it is just the way it was.

What is known was that once again, Michael Telling was terrified of the thought of years in prison, of any time in prison actually. He had had it cushy so far, prisoners on remand have so many more rights that those convicted, such as carpeted cells and outside meals brought in with alcohol. But on conviction, such luxuries stop. Normally. Also access to unlimited funds stops. A convicted criminal in prison has to earn money for minor luxuries such as chocolate of tobacco. Any access to money from the Vestey trust would have to stop, or pause at least on conviction whilst in prison. Those are the rules. All privileges from being on remand would also stop. Time spent on remand in prison is counted as time served in England, and so even a short sentence at worst may ensure his immediate release, if things went well, if George Carmen did the job that he was being so handsomely paid to do and if things went to plan. The perpetrators of domestic killings, manslaughters are frequently sentenced to 'time served', after all.

Telling pleaded not guilty to murder but guilty to manslaughter because of diminished responsibility. Manslaughter can be voluntary or involuntary, depending on the accused's level of *mens rea* (Latin expression which means guilty mind). With diminished responsibility one was incapable of forming a *mens rea*. That would mean sentence at worse would be minimal. Even more so if it could be proven to the judge or jury, or that they could be persuaded that Monika had provoked him into such regretful action. Except that Michael Telling showed no regret.

In law in England, provocation is when a person is considered to have committed a criminal act, partly because of a preceding set of events that might cause a reasonable person to lose self-control. This makes them less morally culpable than if the act was premeditated and carried out from pure malice, or from lust.

The sensational newspaper headlines and articles continued, ever more assiduous daily. Monika's reputation, via the mouthpiece George Carmen was destroyed and reported on. The allegations and reports varied but they included the fact that 'Monika was evil. She only had one thing in mind with however she touched. That was to destroy them and to wreck their lives'. She rode naked into parties on one of Telling's Harley Davidson's, she trained her pet cockatoo to spit and swear (probably true – with the assistance of others), she had a sexual fetish for rubber ducks, there was a non-revealing photograph or Monika in a bath with a rubber duck. The press offered £20,000 for it at the time, she slept with so many men and women that the number would exceed the population of High Wycombe, no man was safe around Monika, and finally that she beat Telling with a whip to satisfy her sexual depravity. None of these salacious stories were ever justified with a shred of proof, and all were from anonymous sources, but of course Monika was dead, and as such she could not answer them. The prosecution at the trial should have given her a voice, but they failed her.

Every man has to be presumed same – capable of forming a criminal intent – if it cannot be proven to the contrary. What Telling did has previously been called an *Irresistible Impulse*. It was a defence attempted in England and rejected in the 1920s, an impulse triggered by jealousy or rage, being pushed beyond the point of human endurance. This defence was accepted in several states in America in the 20s, but not accepted into British law until the 1950s, and the new 1957 Homicide Act. Mental Impairment, temporary insanity became a defence to murder. In such cases, if proven, the defendant cannot be convicted of the crime of murder, and manslaughter is the only safe conviction, the only possible conviction under such circumstances.

But all professionals have differing opinions about

many things. That is not to say that all are corrupt, will say things for reward or for publicity.

It is said, 'Don't let the noise of others' opinions drown out your own inner voice. As long as the reason of man continues fallible, and he is at liberty to exercise it, different opinions will be formed. We meet aliens every day who have something to give us. They come in the form of people with different opinions'.

Psychiatrists are indeed such aliens to most of us, and they differ in opinion greatly, as they certainly did in the case of Regina v Michael Telling at Exeter Crown Court in 1984.

CHAPTER
THIRTY-SEVEN

ON TUESDAY 19TH JUNE 1984, people in US were listening to The Reflex by Duran Duran.

In UK Wake Me Up Before You Go Go by Wham! was in the charts, and The Witches Of Eastwick by John Updike was one of the bestselling books. And in Southernhay Gardens, Exeter Crown Court, the trial on the charge of murder against Michael Telling commenced with the evidence for the prosecution.

Telling had pleaded not guilty to murder but guilty to manslaughter by reason of diminished responsibility. He was immaculately dressed in a bespoke pinstripe suit.

The jury of twelve good men (and women) and true were sworn in. Let the purge commence.

The truth is that people will provoke you until they bring out your ugly side, then play the victim when you go there, as did Michael Telling.

A narcissist will have no qualms in assassinating a person's character. It is an intentional attempt to influence and to cause others to develop an extremely negative opinion of them. They manipulate facts spread lies and slander in order to paint an untrue picture of their target opening up the target for unwarranted and excessive criticism. Michael Telling was such a narcissist, someone who had too much admiration for himself, showing arrogance and contempt for Monika.

Alan Rawley QC was appointed as prosecutor in the trial. He was called to the bar back in 1958, and appointed Queens Council in 1977. An experienced council, his speciality practice was in serious crime. He had strong links to Exeter, and was known to have a particularly easy manner with a jury; he loved jury advocacy. Alan was always prepared to stand up to judges with a straight-talking tenacity.

The opposing council was, as previously stated, George Carmen QC. He was a leading English barrister during the 1980s. In 1979, he had successfully defended the former Liberal leader Jeremy Thorpe after he was charged with conspiracy to murder. Carman had been appointed as a Queen's Counsel eight years previously. His manner was totally different from Alan Rawley, and he was known for his overbearing and confrontational approach.

The judge in the red robes was Sir John Sheldon. At age 71 he was an experienced advocate, barrister, former commissioned officer in the Royal Artillery, High Court Judge, and County Court Judge.

The line up and experience of these three men, who amongst them would either determine or assist in the determination of the fate of Michael Telling that summer in the huge Number Two courtroom at Exeter Crown Court was formidable.

And the trial proper commenced. Alan Rawley started the case for the prosecution. He had decided to read out Telling's confession of the killing, and he made it clear to the jury that the onus was on them to decide on pre-meditation, or if he was mentally ill and therefore could not form the guilty intent to kill.

Court transcripts show that he said, "The jury may think that anyone who kept a body rotting in a summer house must be out of their mind, and anyone who cuts off a head must be out of their mind, but the facts of this case are more complex. It seems that his wife was rather difficult young woman. It also appears that he had experienced emotional problems as a child and may even have experienced a degree of mental impairment at the time he killed his wife. But is for you, members of the jury, to determine if the defendant is guilty of murder. Was this an act of intelligence and cunning, and in equally cunning fashion, did he take elaborate steps to cover up his actions?"

The first witness was called. It was the man named Joe Stennings, allegedly the last person other than Telling to see Monika alive. He knew the couple originally from The Boot public house. He had said that on the day before Monika went into The Chilterns for dental surgery, she had said to Telling, in his presence, "You bought a fucking gun". Telling denied having done so. She mentioned it again, and again Telling denied it. He had been present when Telling had packed for his stay at St. Andrews hospital and witnessed his reticence. He had also seen him the next morning when he had said that he was not going, and that Monika had gone away.

Stennings described Telling as a nice chap, but a man who never listened to what anyone else had to say, that his mind would wander after a few seconds, interrupt and change the subject. He said that in his opinion, Monika sometimes picked on Telling, occasionally saying unnecessary things.

He was not asked about the night that he allegedly spent with Monika, and neither was it mentioned in court.

Then it was the turn of the defence to rebut anything said.

It did not start well. Stennings was able to speak about Telling's affection, love for her and the fact that it was requited by Monika. That was unexpected. He then turned to Monika's alcoholism. Did he know, and if so how long had he known. He had known, and for about a year before she disappeared? Carmen made the statement that Telling was concerned about it, and had tried to stop her, but she did not agree and often drank alone. Stennings disagreed, stating that Monika knew her problems and was dealing with them, and would not drink alone, nor go out of her way to do so. Once again it was not the expected or wanted response.

Carmen then turned to drugs. Stennings said that he was unaware, and had not seen her smoke cannabis, she had never mentioned cocaine, but there were always several bottles of pills about the place. Again, not the response expected.

"Did you know that Monika was a lesbian?". Stennings did not, and he never had any suspicion whatsoever. Again, wrong answer for Carmen.

He then turned to Telling's psychiatric problems. Did Monika insist that he admitted himself as a voluntary patient? He did indeed, and the matter had been raised several times between the two in his presence. Monika was very clearly the dominant partner in the relationship, but Carmen wanted him to say more. "Is it not true that she picked on him sometimes, more than was necessary?"

Stennings answered that he did not agree with that, in his opinion she did not pick on him but they argued, bickered with him, and agreed that she was sometimes critical of him. He then asked a couple of questions relating to the dogs that Telling had acquired after Monika's disappearance and had no further questions for Mr Stennings.

The next witness called was Cheryl Richardson. It did not go well for the prosecution case. She said that Monika smoked cannabis and although hearsay, Michael Telling had told her that she took cocaine. Monika enjoyed humiliating Telling, taunting him about his sexual inadequacy. That Monika had told her that she was a lesbian, and that "if she screwed me I would never want another man". She had taken lesbians back to Lambourne House while Telling was there. She enjoyed humiliating Michael Telling.

Michael Telling's mother the former Joyce Vestey, now Joyce Strong now living in Australia was next. She had never met Monika, her daughter in law. She told the story of his disturbed childhood, and said that she had only ever spoken to Monika once on the telephone. She had formed the opinion from that brief conversation that Monika was, 'hard'.

But she was able to tell the stories of her son, to whom she had never shown any motherly love. She told tales of how he chased other children with matches, how he almost died from eating stolen sweets, and even how he broke a bottle over a girls head, amongst other things. But none of this was her fault though. Like mother like son.

The next day, 21st June, in their usual fashion, The Sun sensationalised the story with the by-line of 'MY WILD, WILD SON'. She had not had one good thing to say about Monika, the girl she had not know, and never would.

Character assassination, and the person being assassinated could not answer back. The dead can tell no tales, they say, and unfortunately, they can not answer back either..

CHAPTER
THIRTY-EIGHT

THE ASSASSINATION CONTINUED.

It was exactly the stuff that George Carman thrived on. Scandal. So many allegations, so many things said that could never be forgotten, Monika Zumsteg had been unlawfully killed that was for sure, and now her reputation was also being killed, and no-one was able to rebut the stories.

One has to wonder who was on trial here, but the answer should be obvious. A student at High Wycombe College of Further Education, Julie Chamberlain stated on oath that she had visited Lambourne House, smoked marijuana with Monika, and that they had kissed and fondled, and spent the night having sex. David Wells and the them Christina Perry were asked about the arguments at Tunbridge Wells, of the bannister destruction by Telling, and Telling's threat to kill Monika if she ever left him. The witnesses were halted if they deviated even slightly from the questioning, and were not allowed to state other things that they considered relevant, the onus, the blame for everything being shifted from Telling to Monika. The witnesses found Carmen both rude and patronising.

Two local women, having met Telling over the CB airways were able to describe the passionate, sometimes inadequate or impossible sex whilst Monika lay dead nearby. Their names were Linda Blackstock and Susan Bright. I have been unable to trace either of them. The man who repaired the telephone line testified to seeing the rifle, and Alison Telling testified as to the gift of the Cartier necklace shortly after Monika's disappearance. Jeff Henthorne testified as to Telling's arrest and subsequent admission, and to the discovery of Monika's head, and many others testified within that first week. Each time the blame was placed firmly upon the victim.

The normally conservative, some may say staid Bucks Free Press, the local High Wycombe newspaper had the lurid and tempting headlines, "TALES OF LESBIAN LOVERS, DRUGS AND ALCOHOL....THEN THREE FATAL SHOTS". However, the headlines and the trial witnessed by reporter Bob Perrin seemed to be somewhat at odds.

He wrote -

> 'From the start of the trial a week ago, it has been Monika Telling, not Michael who has been stalked by one of the greatest legal minds in the world, George Carmen, QC. One by one the witnesses come forward to tell in their various ways the ways that their lives crossed the star touched Tellings. To begin with they are led through their evidence by the

council prosecuting for The Crown, Alan Rawley, QC, a squirrel like figure, gregarious and generously built. Then, quietly, again and again, Mr Carmen rises to consider what they have said. He is a small man, owl like in profile, a tiny white scar on his left cheek, beautifully spoken. He never refers to Michael Telling as the accused, never looks at him behind the serried ranks of lawyers, flanked by two prison warders. No, to everyone, Mr Carmen talks of Michael this and Michael that. As the hours pass by, you – and probably the jury – begin to think of him as someone close, an acquaintance of some standing, a victim. It is a lawyer's trick, one of his many, and you marvel at his skills".

The drunken, money grabber, seeking his fortune was on trial. The delirium continued, unabated, seemingly insatiable.

Monika Zumsteg was on trial here, and certainly not the killer; her killer, Michael Telling.

CHAPTER
THIRTY-NINE

THE UNSTOPPABLE AND uncensorable British press wanted to sell newsprint, at whatever, whoever's cost.

But one newspaper whose contribution has previously been reported put it more succinctly, more sensible and in more measured and non-sensational terms.

It read-

'It would be an exaggeration to call this the murder trial of the century but certainly few have contained so many ingredients of a blood and lust best seller. There in the dock sits a chubby, rather timid man, Michael Telling, the rejected and stunted sprig of a mighty family tree. Grandson of the incredibly wealthy first Lord Vestey, he was born with a silver albatross around his neck. He married a pleasant, everyday woman and he was unable, as she put it, to shoulder the responsibilities of being a husband and father. Then from her safe arms he drops into the talons of a woman who has surely become one of the most celebrated wicked ladies in the history of British jurisprudence – his second wife Monika'.

John Hamilton had classed him, Telling, as a 'cold blooded, calculated and sane killer'.

Hamilton had said in court that his initial impression of Telling was that of, 'he was an extremely talkative man and it was difficult to get him to stop talking. The essence of his talking was to portray himself in the best possible light, and to portray his victim, Monika, in the worst possible light'. He added that Telling was co-operative but had attempted to steer the conversation his way and was less than truthful.

He stated that Telling had admitted to having formed the intention to kill Monika some time before he carried it out, that he formed the intent to kill her when she returned from her hospital appointment, the next day. He said that Telling had made the decision to shoot her. He stated his belief that Telling was quite capable of making rational decisions and judgements and was able to control his impulses – if he wished to do so. He believed that if the decision to shoot Monika had been a spur of the moment decision, not premeditated, that on firing the first shot, he would have been shocked out if his fugue, and not reloaded and shot her several more times.

He believed that the actions underlined the cold-blooded and calculated way that he killed her. His hiring a private detective, emptying her bank account, keeping the body, the burial and the removal of the head were all cold and calculated actions of a 'cunning and clever man' who knew exactly what he was doing, and that his actions rebutted what he had told the police, that he could not bear to leave her all there because he loved her. He finally agreed that Telling had an abnormality of his mind, a personality disorder but of a moderate degree, but not such an abnormality to impair his mental responsibility for his acts.

The judge spoke. "Let me get this right. As I understand this position, he did have a personality disorder, but it was one of a moderate degree?" Hamilton agreed. The judge said, "Does that mean that you believe the personality disorder was not severe enough to substantially impair his actions under the Homicide Act of 1957?". Hamilton agreed. There would be a short recess, after which, Mr Carmen had a few questions for him.

Everything he said was rebutted by the defence, by George Carmen in his cross examination.

The degree of Tellings personality disorder was at the forefront, the most important part of the definition of and the difference between murder and manslaughter, and how severe or moderate his abnormality was. The eminent witness for the prosecution had previously published a paper on the impact of Adolf Hitler's father had upon the tyrant, and as such was able to distinguish in matters of intent. He insisted that Telling was cunning, selfish and manipulative. A man who knew what he was doing, and had the ability to stop himself, had he wished to do so.

He was asked if he felt that Telling was abnormal. He answered that he did consider him to be an abnormal man, but one with only a mild personality disorder. Hamilton considered that the proper course of action for the couple would have been divorce, not murder, and he expressed his opinion. He was asked if he considered, given the trauma of his upbringing, that 'Something would go seriously wrong in his adult life'. "Is it not true that the sins of the fathers are visited upon the children?" "No". "Would be correct to say, that as a child Michael Telling was profoundly disturbed?"

"He was disturbed, yes".

"That is not what I asked you. I asked if he was profoundly disturbed?"

"He was profoundly disturbed", he agreed.

Carmen then turned to the witness's knowledge of Tellings family. The Vestey's. He admitted, as most of the country did to not knowing much about them.

He was told that on his coming of age, he would become the heir to a vast fortune. "How would the affect a man considered to be somewhat a failure to the family, a man who had achieved nothing in life?"

"It would certainly be a bad thing for him". He agreed that it would indeed become a handicap.

Then Carmen described Monika as a 'fun seeking, drug taking, promiscuous Californian", and that it was obvious that the two of them together were the very worst possible mix. Hamilton had to agree.

At this stage, one would be forgiven in thinking

that the prosecuting council, Alan Rawley, may have objected to the damning of Monika, but he did not. His job was to convict Michael Telling, not to defend the reputation of Monika, however damning that may become.

Carmen referred to Hamilton's notes. He said that he was unable to find in those handwritten notes, several things that had been said at court by him. Much was made that no note was taken of Telling's alleged confession that he had intended to kill her when they were at the Hyde Park Hotel, but Hamilton was able to find a passage where he said that Telling told him that 'the seeds were sown' then. Telling had also said of Monika, 'if I can't have her no one else will' and that he had decided to kill her.

Carmen insisted that if Telling had admitted as such that his words would have been recorded contemporaneously, and that his recollection was at fault.

The judge interjected at this point, asking if Hamilton had any doubt whatsoever that Telling told him that he had decided to kill Monika whilst at the Hyde Park Hotel. Hamilton replied that he had no doubt at all.

He was excused, and the prosecution case rested. Next it was time for the defence. Telling was seen with a pile of papers before him, occasionally scribbling notes and passing them to the bevy of lesser barristers for the defence sitting dutifully behind their masters.

The game was very much afoot.

CHAPTER
FORTY

THE DEFENCE HAD many people to call, the first of which was, 53 year old professor Robert Bluglass later to become a CBE, emeritus professor of forensic psychology at Birmingham university, and clinical director, Reaside clinic in Birmingham.

But today he was a rebuttal witness in a murder trial. This was not his first time in court, indeed he had testified in over four hundred cases before.

His opinion on Telling was asked. Was his state of mind capable of forming the intent to murder? "In my opinion he suffered an abnormality of mind as a child, and also suffered an abnormality of mind at the time of his wife's death". His opinion was that Telling had a severe personality disorder. He went on to say that he believed that Telling was of diminished responsibility at the time of the killing, and as such, Dr Hamilton was incorrect, wrong in his assessment.

Carmen then took a similar tract as before. He went over things he had already done. Telling came from a deprived and unloved childhood, was bullied and troubled, and that his victim was an alcoholic and drug taking lesbian. It was a statement more than a question. He then asked the witness what he thought the attraction of Monika was to Telling.

Bluglass replied that he considered Monika the opposite of Alison who was 'homely'. He thought that Monika was attractive, exciting and dominating. Bluglass had never met Monika, but it appears that he was eminently qualified to comment on her state of mind, if she actually loved her killer. With no objection forthcoming, he stated his opinion that he believed her to be a disturbed personality herself, and that her feelings were not those of love and affection, her criticism of him showed as much.

His actions after he had killed her proved Telling's devotion to his wife. The fact that he had said he could not leave her all in Devon showed that. The fact that he cut off her head with an axe, and brought the head back to Lambourne House in plastic bags, and later added maggots to speed up the decomposition proved as much.

After the lunch break, he was asked about the negative impact on his development that his childhood had on him. His father attacked his mother, and his mother showed little or no affection towards him. He became attached to various nannies, who were frequently dismissed, sent away. He was sent away, rejected again. When he stole to get home to see his mother she simply sent him back again, rejected once more. He felt that Monika with her domineering personality was similar to his mother, and he sought her love and acceptance, and once again he was put down verbally and again rejected.

His fascination with firearms was a sign to Michael Telling of his masculinity, and just like his cars and motorcycles and other possessions, represented a power to him.

No mention of his previous convictions. No mention of his previous violence, just evidence of a misunderstood man. In his opinion, Michael Telling was far from the opinion that Dr Hamilton had of him. "He is a man of mixed and considerable emotions who acts on impulse, not on planning nor calculation". He further stated that he did not believe Telling's alleged admission to his intent to kill Monika at the Hyde Park Hotel in Knightsbridge.

"No more questions for this witness", said George Carmen.

Now it was time for the prosecution to rebut the testimony that had been given.

CHAPTER
FORTY-ONE

BLUGLASS THEN FACED cross examination from the prosecution.

He admitted that he had strangely formed his opinion on Telling's mental state having listened to other witnesses describe his attitude, his actions.

He was reminded that Dr Hamilton had stated on oath that Telling had admitted to him that his intent to kill Monika was formed at the Hyde Park Hotel. Bluglass said that he did not accept it, that he did not believe that it was true. He thought Telling incapable of giving a clear and truthful account, of knowing exactly when he formed the intent to kill Monika, and that in his opinion he only formed the intent the morning that he killed her, when he actually picked up the gun, and he lost his temper and shot her.

And even if the intent was formed earlier, Telling was a man with substantial diminished responsibility. Of that he had "no doubt at all". Even if what Hamilton had said about his admission of intent at the

Hyde Park Hotel, he would not change his opinion, that Monika had provoked him into killing her. Her death was her fault. He further once again said that he believed that Telling had kept the body in the sauna for five months because he could not bear to leave her, to be parted from her and he wanted her close to him. He did not believe that Telling had kept her body simply to attempt to cover up his crime. He stated that he believed that the act of cutting her head off with the convenient axe was an act of impulse, a spur of the moment act. Telling had said so, and he believed him. He loved her and wanted to take some of her back home.

Rawley asked about the fact that he had taken the axe with him, and additionally taken plastic bags to put the head in, evidence of intent. Bluglass said that he did not know the answer to that.

As always, Michael Telling had an answer for everything. He passed a scrawled note to the defence minions with his answer to that. It read, 'It's a matter of course (sic). When I travel I always take bags with me. I took some to Monte Carlo, Australia, USA for rubbish, dirty washing etc.'

Rawley then asked the most pertinent question of Bluglass. "Supposing he had done it in order to disguise the identity of the corpse and take the head away so that if the corpse was found they still would not know who it is. In such case it would have been a very cold, determined, planned course of conduct. Couldn't this simply be a case in which an irate husband decided, out of revenge, jealousy, or any other motive that springs from an unhappy marriage, to get rid of a wife he no longer wanted. Wasn't everything part of the same pattern – a calculated, premeditated murder followed by a resourceful and effective cover up by a manipulative liar".

Of course, it was. But Bluglass simply answered "No".

It was next the turn of the next witness for the defence. This was the eminent physiatrist, Dr Paul Bowden, a forensic psychiatrist at the Bethlem Royal and Maudsley hospitals in London. The criminal courts made extensive use of his expertise, often in high-profile trials. His experience, interests and personality helped make him an effective teacher who shaped the skills and outlook of many of the senior figures within British forensic psychiatry. And star witness for the defence of Michael Telling.

Not unlike the previous witness, he agreed with what had been said. "He was a man who wanted things immediately or even quicker", he stated. The shooting of Monika was guided by an invisible force, over which he had no control. The issue had occurred because of his traumatic childhood.

In cross examination he agreed that Telling was a manipulative man, a man intent on blaming others for his very great shortcomings, and those of Monika. He interviewed or examined Telling in Exeter prison, and admitted that he, Telling, had attempted to manipulate the session and the thoughts of Bowden, that a custodial prison sentence was the incorrect course of action for him, and that he acted like a spoilt child and when he did not get his own way, he became threatening. He wrote in his notes '….He was unwilling or unable to consider his own contribution to his predicament, intent only on gaining maximum publicity for his account of Monika's shortcomings'. He agreed that Telling was manipulative but that his opinion stood, Telling was of substantially diminished responsibility.

His opinion was the contention of the prosecution that the removal of the head and its concealment at Lambourne house was an effort to cover up the identity, and to avoid arrest.

Rawley pushed further. " …Even if the defendant had an abnormality of mind, was it not likely that he still possessed sufficient willpower when he killed his wife that it was wrong, and not to pull the trigger?"

Bowden disagreed there. He said, "No".

Rawley then suggested that there could be no doubt that Telling knew what he was doing when he killed Monika. Bowden agreed with that contention.

Rawley then suggested that there could be no doubt that Telling knew the difference between right and wrong and in any case had the ability to make a rational judgement. Bowden disagreed. He said that the question of right or wrong probably never entered Telling's mind, that he never applied the question to himself, to what he was doing.

On further cross examination, Bowden said that his opinion was that Telling was, "…in such an abnormal state that the strength of the impulse to shoot Monika was irresistible, one that he was incapable of fighting.

Rawley pushed. Wasn't Telling just doing what he wanted to do, "come hell or high water". Wasn't he simply refusing to accept what he knew was so wrong, and choosing not to exert any will power? If indeed that was the case, it follows that he is NOT suffering in that possible situation from diminished responsibility?

The definition of diminished responsibility in law is, 'an unbalanced mental state that is considered to make a person less answerable for a crime and to be grounds for a reduced charge, but that does not classify them as insane'.

Rawley suggested that an irresistible impulse would not account for planning the killing days before the act.

The irresistible impulse would not account for purchasing or picking up the gun and walking around with it. Bowden stated that he doubted that Telling would have been unable to resist the feelings that he had. That he would not have been able to have any control over any decision to pick up the gun.

Time and time again, under cross examination, Bowden disagreed with the prosecutor in his contentions. Even when he took the loaded weapon, shot Monika, he could not resist the impulse to reload and shoot again. And then reload and shoot again, and again.

The final point made by Mr Rawley was that from his initial decision to kill Monika, Telling could have changed his mind at any time, but he chose not to do so.

The answer was not as expected. " I am saying that his strength of feeling was such that he could not, even if he tried, exercise control over his physical actions". He could not have stopped himself from killing Monika.

That was the last question for the witness and he was dismissed, excused.

He had been the final witness.

A defendant in a criminal trial in England has no obligation to answer any questions, but may choose whether or not to give evidence in the proceedings. It is sometimes referred to as the privilege against self-incrimination. Telling, or his substantial council chose for him not to give evidence. They clearly thought that enough had been said.

What other reason could there possibly have been for his silence?

CHAPTER
FORTY-TWO

WHAT WAS NEVER in contention was that Telling rated an impressive eight out of ten on a scale of evil.

It was on an accepted scale, based on Attila the Hun rated at ten and Saint Frances of Assisi zero.

It was normal practice for both the prosecution and defence to summarise the case before the jury. There was really only one question in contention. There was no doubt that Telling had killed Monika, but what was his mental state at the time? Was it a planned and calculated act, or was it a result of a broken, abnormal and deranged mind acting on the spur of the moment, and unable to control his impulses?

Rawley pointed to the amazing lengths that Telling had gone to, to cover up. He had lied about Monika leaving him, employed a private detective, destroyed the gun and axe, installed security at Lambourne House, purchased dogs, planted conifers, and used powerful air purifiers to cover up the smell. The whole thing was planned with an elaborate story to justify burying the body, and removing the head to avoid detection. "Despite any mental abnormality this man was determined to kill his wife". He continued in expressing how mentally sick the defendant was, "How can you, unless you have a severely disordered personality, bring back your own child to that very house where the rotting body lay? Heavens above, you must have felt moments of sympathy for Michael Telling, mixed with the horror of what he did. A manslaughter verdict would be a true one, not one of sympathy"

George Rawley pulled upon the heartstrings of the jury, saying that if they found Telling guilty of murder that they would, "deliver him a final and ultimate rejection". He continued the story, "He had all the money in the world, but nowhere to go and no-one to love. He was the inadequate black sheep of the family. No achievements, he did not even have a home.

In the Crown Courts it was now the turn of the judge to sum up the case and the evidence, and to clarify points of law in all that had been presented to them in more simple language, in order that they could rightly consider all the facts, and to totally understand what they had witnessed over the past eight days. He stated that there was no doubt that Telling had killed Monika, but it was up to the jury to determine why. It had taken six hours to sum up the case for the prosecution, the defence and the judge, Mr Justice Sheldon.

His summary was succinct and could never be questioned.

The decision was now one for the jury to make.

Was the man before them guilty of murder or manslaughter? Was he capable of murder, or was he simply a man who had had a loveless childhood and was himself a victim? These twelve people, seven men and five women would have to decide, but whatever they did decide, the media frenzy would continue, and even before the verdict was delivered, a guilty verdict had been delivered, on Monika.

The red top Daily Star led with Telling's story of woe, 'SLAVE OF THE VAMP', while others reported, 'I GUNNED DOWN HORRIBLE WIFE, and 'THE SAD TALE OF THE POOR LITTLE RICH BOY AND THE WICKED LADY', and the ever true Sun went to town with 'I WANT YOU FOR MY SEX SANDWICH'. The Express led with a special. 'THE HELL OF LIFE WITH MONIKA- THE BIZARRE STORY OF MILLIONAIRE MICHAEL TELLING AND THE HEADLESS CORPSE CASE' The Times was somewhat more restrained, 'MILLIONAIRE'S COUSIN KILLED AND BEHEADED WIFE AFTER SEXUAL TAUNTS'.

Exactly two hours and thirty six minutes after retiring to consider the verdict, the jury were back. They had reached a decision, a decision that would alter lives. The unanimous decision was:

"Not guilty of murder, but guilty of manslaughter by reason of diminished responsibility". Once again, Telling had won. Before the judge passed sentence on the grinning defendant, George Carmen said, "he has instructed me he would wish to express to Your Lordship his appreciation of the terrible thing he has done in the taking away the life of his own wife, who he loved dearly". Of course he did. Her killing and the subsequent killing of her reputation to suit his own means had surely proven that. Carmen's further suggestion that prison was not the correct sentence fell on deaf ears.

The judge was clearly unimpressed with this late show of contrition.

"Michael Henry Maxwell Telling. The jury have found you guilty of manslaughter by reason of diminished responsibility. There was ample evidence on which they could do so, including, in particular, the evidence of Professor Bluglass and doctor Bowden. Accordingly, just as I accept the jury's verdict, I must have regard to their evidence in considering sentence. In my opinion it would be unpleasant and unkind of me to repeat the evidence of your past, present and likely future mental state. Suffice it to say, it must clearly be the case that that you have matured very little from the profoundly disturbed little boy that you were in your early life, and that the prognosis for the future is bleak. With little or no greater ability now, to control your emotions and impulses. That is the evidence that the jury have accepted, and the evidence upon which I must act.

In those circumstances, I am satisfied that there can be no alternative to passing a sentence, as I do, of life imprisonment, thus leaving it to those responsible for your custody to decide whether, and if so, when it should be safe and proper to permit your release".

Telling was visibly shocked at the unnecessary severity of the sentence, but he was alone in thinking so. Neither the prosecution nor defence were.

Michael Telling was led out of the courtroom to

begin his sentence as a convicted killer. He ordered his usual restaurant meal and wine to be brought in to the prison, as he had done on remand, and was shocked to be told that as a convicted man he no longer had any privileges.

He would live as everyone else did, eat the same food, and comply with the rules, maybe for life.

But this bizarre story was far from finished. Michael Telling was nowhere near finished yet.

CHAPTER
FORTY-THREE
MEMORIES OF MONIKA – CHRISTINA FINLAYSON NEE PERCY

"I FIRST MET *Monika at the Grange public house, Langton. She had been for a horse-riding lesson and had stopped there for some lunch.*

She was playing pool and I asked her for a game. Then we struck up a conversation. She was a warm & genuinely friendly person, and made people feel at ease straight away.

We arranged to meet the following week and she invited myself and my boyfriend back to her house for coffee and lunch. She told us that Michael, her husband (although they were not married at this point) was away on business, but we would meet him soon.

A couple of weeks later we met Michael, who told us immediately that he was in the SAS and had been away on a secret mission. At first that sounded impressive of course. I was young and had never met anyone like this before.

But in reality, he was not an SAS soldier, in fact he did not work at all, and had been away to Devon to see his first wife & son. He was about to divorce his wife, and he could not marry Monika until the divorce was final. Monika did not know this at the time.

We did go out for many meals to either pizza places, or expensive restaurants and Michael always paid, usually flashing his Amex card! Monika was so kind. She leant me clothes and expensive jewellery. I was only 20 and had not long started work for the Nat West Bank.

She made friends very easily because, she was down to earth, never snobby and could relate to any class of people, something which Michael could not. He had no friends but only gold diggers who flocked around him like bees around a honey pot, when he pulled wads of cash from his wallet. This was the only way he would have people talk to him.

Of course, he told such tall stories and made up things to impress others. Monika did try to help & educate him but he would not have it.

He was extremely jealous of her ability to make new friends and the fact that she was very intelligent. She worked at Reynold & Reynolds in computing. As I worked in a bank we kinda had a connection right from the start.

All Michael was really interested in was Harley - Davidson motor cycles and bragging about how much things cost, and how money was no object, something which Monika didn't like.

She was not born with a silver spoon in her mouth. She came from a respectful family and had values. She would give you her last penny if it would help you. She, so much unlike Michael had to work hard for a living and therefore appreciated everything she had, and had learned from her parents.

Michael was a type 1 diabetic but didn't look after himself that well. On several occasions when his bloods were out of sync, he would start an argument and had the most dreadful temper. One time he demolished the whole banister in the rented house they first stayed in in Poona Road in Tunbridge Wells. That night there was a dreadful storm and torrential rain and after he had thrown bits of the bannister downstairs at myself and Monika, he took a gun and disappeared into the night, threatening to kill himself.

He eventually returned home hours later and all was calm. I had gone home to my own house by then, but Monika told me this.

I was scared for Monika. He really was a bully and when he couldn't get his own way, like a spoilt child he would argue, sulk and then do something irrational for attention.

I was asked by Monika to be her maid of honour at their wedding. Michael gave us £500 cash each and off we went to London, to Harrods and to other shops to get what we needed, what we wanted. She was always so generous. Monika bought me a silk skirt, blouse and a hat, plus pieces for my hair. I had never seen that much money except in the bank. But she didn't squander it and bought several things at bargain prices. Even though she could have asked for more and spent it all, she did not.

She was always collecting little freebies when she was out. Little jars of preserves or English honey. The kind you bought as a souvenir. She would box them up and send them home to her mum, so thoughtful.

Monika was just as happy if not more to shop at a bargain store rather than Harrods, she definitely was not a snob in any way.

I was 21 in Dec 1982 and they had been away to Morocco for a holiday. I had invited them to my party in Tunbridge Wells but didn't think they would come. They arrived back that day from Morocco at 6 am, but still at around 8.30 pm they arrived at the party, they had driven from Radnage to come to my party. She never let me down. That's what true friends are for. Michael wouldn't have bothered but she insisted. I am sure the buffet I had wasn't what he was used to but Monika said the party was lovely and so was the food.

When they moved to Lambourne house, I spent many weekends there and often went to antique fayres on Sunday mornings in Thame & Chinnor. She taught herself about antiques by reading lots of books, and it did not take her long before she was buying and selling.

She was friendly with a guy named David who owned an antique shop in Beaconsfield and was always calling in there to see what new pieces he had. Michael had no interest at all. In fact, he had very little interest in anything except himself and his motorbikes and cars, he never worked in his life. He spent hours on his CB radio, a trend at the time.

Considering the class of family that he was born into, he always attracted the wrong class of people to mix with. Probably because he was of such low intelligence or intellect, these were the only kind of people he could relate too. These people were scroungers and gold diggers, easily impressed with someone with obvious wealth. I was working class but I had had a reasonable education and I had a good job. I met some very high-class customers and I learnt early on how to communicate with them and be discrete. But Michael did not possess any qualities in that respect.

He used to kiss Monika's forehead and stroke her hair as if she was a pet. He used to show her off and brag how lucky he was to have such a beauty. Just a shame he didn't treat her very well".

PART ONE

"When Monika first arrived in Tunbridge Wells, she took a job as a saleswoman for a company called Betterware. She was a natural saleswoman. I went around with her at the weekend collecting brochures and delivering orders. She really enjoyed earning her own money. She was fiercely independent and did not want to rely on Michael asking for money.

One time after she had been in the UK for a couple of months, she had parked her VW Golf on double yellow lines in the High St. As we returned to the car, the traffic warden was about to put a ticket on the car. She put on her best smile, told him she was a tourist and apologised profusely for breaking the law. She promised she would study the Highway code! The warden let her off. As we drove away, she laughed and so did I. Only she could have pulled that one off and got away with it. She had a wonderful sense of humour. In fact, we both had quite warped, wacky senses of humour. Probably why we got on so well.

At their wedding in Nov 1981, there were only a few people. But I remember her parents who were lovely people and the grandparents who were so sweet. She adored them. There was a small reception back at the house afterwards. They went away later to a hotel in Hyde Park and I stayed at the house with her family and looked after them as I knew where things were.

I so enjoyed the Antique Fayres on Sunday mornings. She had interesting things to sell and also bought from other stalls. I really learned a lot from her.

In Tunbridge Wells, she took me to this lady's house where I learnt to play Back Gammon. She was an excellent player and she taught me well. I still play online against players from all over the world. I get told that I am a great player. I owe that to Monika who taught me.

As time went on, Monika became increasingly frustrated with Michael. She tried to educate him but he wouldn't have it. His choice of friends was dire. She had decided in the end she wanted a divorce. She started saving small amounts of money to buy herself a ticket back to the states. She stashed this little black pouch in her wardrobe.

One day, in an argument, he ransacked her wardrobe, found her money bag and burnt it in front of her. She asked him for a divorce and he refused.

He was obsessed with her and really if he couldn't have her, then he would make sure no one else would have her!

In March of 1982, Monika had to go into hospital to have surgery on her teeth. This was at the Private Hospital in Great Missenden. I phoned the hospital and managed to speak with her but she was very groggy. I felt very sorry for her at this time.

I couldn't get through after that. Her phone was disconnected. But she wrote me a letter telling me, that Michael whilst she was in hospital had had the removal van in and moved most of the furniture out. She had no idea where he was, that he had purchased more guns illegally at Christmas of 1981 and she was scared.

I went with my boyfriend that weekend of the 19th March and drove to Lambourne House. She was very scared but so pleased to see us when she opened the door. She bolted it so no one could get in.

Michael later telephoned, as she had managed to get the phone back at 5am. He said he was in Australia! We never knew why.

That weekend was the last weekend I ever saw her. Michael changed the phone number so we couldn't get through. I rang the Boot public house and left a message. He did telephone me and said Monika had returned to the USA. I didn't really believe this as found it strange she hadn't made contact.

Monika was a good friend and I knew something was wrong as she would not have just forgotten me.

Michael rang again and invited myself and my boyfriend to the house for the weekend. He said he had electric gates fitted and dogs now. I had a very strange feeling about the whole thing and made my excuses not to visit before hanging up.

Eventually one evening in September, a news item came on the television. A body had been found, and I recognised the T shirt it was dressed in. I knew in my heart then what had happened, and I went to my local police station and gave a statement. It was a horrible ordeal for me and was upset for years.

The trial in 1984 was a terrible experience for me, and I still have it fresh in my mind. As I entered the court, Michael was standing in the dock, looked at me and smiled.

During the whole trial, Monika's good name was dragged through the mud. Her character was assassinated. I tried to give my side of the story in court but was shot down in flames by his defence barrister, George Carman, both rude and patronising

After Michael was sentenced, I spent years looking over my shoulder, worried in case one day he would come looking for me. Even after I married and moved a long way away to Scotland in 1993, I regularly thought about him and was scared in case he found me.

When I eventually got the internet, I looked online for any information but it was very scarce at that time. In January 2010, I googled his name and there a huge picture of him popped up. I was nearly sick. When I read the article, it said he was in Australia and had died in Dec 2009. I cried with relief. I knew that he could never find me or harm me then.

I have never forgotten my beautiful friend Monika and not a day goes by when she doesn't enter my mind. I only wish, I had had enough money to give her when she wanted to leave and then she could have escaped and who knows how different things might have been.

Rest in peace my wonderful friend and fly with the Angels forever."

RIKI ZUMSTEG MEMORIES :

The Zumsteg family

It is important to give a glimpse of Monika, and our family. Who we were, and how we grew up.

I am Erika Zumsteg-Bedford. Family, and friends have always referred to me as "Riki". I am a fraternal twin to my brother Mark Zumsteg. Monika was our older sister by six years. Mom is Elsa, and our Dad is Lou.

Mom was born during the depression in (1929) Switzerland, and raised during the war. Dad was born in Oakland, CA. USA (1930). They met each other at a German restaurant where mom was a waitress.

It was like a Hollywood movie. A young handsome man in a military uniform, notices a lovely woman, and decides then.... "this is the woman I'm going to marry"! Eventually, Dad won my mother's heart, and they married Oct. 1955. .

Monika was born November 1956 in Oakland, CA. on Dad's birthday. He was so happy. Every year they shared a special day. Being the first grandchild, Monika was such a wonderful surprise to my grandmother. She had raised two boys, and welcomed the opportunity to be a grandma to a little girl.

Mark, and I were born in New Orleans LA. three days before Dad, and Monika's birthdays (twins). The family had relocated there, because Dad was transferred by Boeing.

We were raised Catholic, celebrated holidays, Dad worked 9-5 with Boeing, and later Schlage Lock Co. Mom was always present, and available. We were taught to earn the things that we wanted, and be proud of our achievements. Dad could be quite strict at times, on the other hand, could be loving, and he certainly had a sense of humour. He, and Monika were often playing and joking together.

Monika, was the "big" sister. I am sure there were times, she wished otherwise....as most older siblings may. For the most part, Monika was a great big sister. She joked, and laughed a lot. (how I loved her laugh) especially if it was a "gotcha" moment... which she, and Dad were very good at. Mark, and I loved being around our sister. We trusted her, and felt safe with Monika.

Monika loved school, and was very intelligent. During High school, her teacher contacted our mother to say, they had nothing left to teach Monika. So, Monika began helping at the nearby middle school, even teaching gymnastics, until she could begin attending college. When Monika first began school at the age of 4, Mom was asked to take Monika out of her kindergarten class, that she was disrupting other children. Monika at four years old had taught herself to read. The disruption?....She was reading to the other children.

Later, Monika began attending school in San Mateo, CA., got a job, her first used car, and moved out on her own. She took our old Black and White Zenith TV with. It would become a symbol of humble beginnings. (until Michael replaced it without her permission).

In the summer of 1976, the family moved to Santa Rosa, CA. Eventually, Monika ended up in the Sacramento area, with a good job, friends, staying in regular contact with our parents, Grandparents, and always home for the holidays. Monika loved Christmas! She spent time making special gifts for everyone. We were raised to believe "It is the thought that counts". I looked forward to every visit, or get-together with my sister. The silly jokes, her natural energy, and fun family stories. She lit up the room, were ever she was.

THE MEETING

It was a beautiful day in Santa Rosa Ca. Truly lovely morning for a motorcycle ride to Sausalito, on the Marin County side of the San Francisco Bay.

I liked riding with my Dad. He had taught both my brother Mark, and I to ride off road when we were 14. I was now 18, and riding a street bike.

After suiting up, we headed out. I was riding my 74 Honda 350 four (Gertrude), Dad, and Mom on the Yamaha 1100 (Genghis) and another couple on their bike. Dad always gave names to his cars, and motorcycles.

We had a smooth ride on highway 101 south, through Sonoma and Marin counties, eventually leaving the highway for the Sausalito exit. As we came to a stop sign near the ferry terminal, my father noticed a man on a new Harley Davidson. Dad loved motorcycles, had several of his own. This one caught his eye. It was a new 1980 Harley Davidson Sturgis, first one to have a belt drive.

It is common for bikers on all makes of motorcycles, to wave to each other on the road, and develop conversations with complete strangers, over their machines. A type of Camaraderie. So, it was not a surprise when the man on the Harley, pulled over in a parking area alongside our bikes. This is the moment when we met Michael Henry Maxwell Telling.

The gentleman biker with a proper English accent, introduced himself. Michael Telling, a tourist from the UK. He had just purchased the Harley from Dudley Perkins Jr. In the City, with a plan to ship the bike back to England.

He was invited by my father to join us for lunch, and a walk through the touristy area of Sausalito. Later, to an outdoor flea market of many vendors. While walking with Michael, we came across a table full of beautiful rocks, and gemstones. Among the display, I was admiring the opals. "Do you like opals"? Michael asked. "Yes" I replied.

As the day reached later into the afternoon, it was time to part ways with the English biker. Dad seemed to enjoy the meeting, and offered for him to visit Santa Rosa, tour the vineyards, and enjoy some beautiful ride time, before his return to the UK.

My father was an outgoing, and social type. Could pick up a conversation with just about anybody. He was a leader, and a teacher, in many ways. Having overcome alcoholism... not a soused bum, but a functional alcoholic, he had become a strong Program member. Creating, and running groups of recovery, and even a motorcycle group The Dry Riders. Often, he would have motorcycle/Program friends around.

The following weekend, the throaty sound of a Harley Davidson came up the drive. It was the seemingly, proper Englishman Michael Telling.

It was not long before Michael asked to take me to dinner. I agreed, and we enjoyed a bite at a local Chinese restaurant. Later that evening, we went to a movie theatre. While waiting in line, Michael pulled out a fancy dark Pink, velvet box. It was a well made gold chain, and gold pendant designed around an Australian opal.

Recalling our walk through the Sausalito market...

"Do you like opals"? Michael asked. "Yes" I replied.

JUST FRIENDS

During Michael's visit, we went on a few rides. One in particular, was to a Napa Valley Winery, and vineyards.

Many Estate wines, and souvenirs. Noticing some handmade beeswax candles, formed into various shapes, I moved closer for a better view. Michael found a Koala bear, and decided to purchased it for me. About $60, which to me, was expensive. It was becoming apparent, that this gentleman was trying to impress me.

Michael asked me to join him, as a passenger on his Harley one morning. He wanted me to accompany him to San Francisco. He drove well, and was comfortable motoring around the "City by the Bay".

The Harley was a marvellous piece of American

Machinery. In honour of the famous Sturgis motorcycle rally, Harley released the Harley-Davidson FXB Sturgis. "B" for Belt drive. First time used by HD.

By Late morning, we arrived at the San Francisco Gun Exchange (no longer in business).

I was raised with guns. Dad, liked to collect, target shoot, and reload ammunition for guns. Mark, and I had been taught young to shoot riffles. We liked to search for spent shells at the range, for Dad to reload. My father had a small collection of guns. First generation Colt 45 revolver, Pepperbox, among others. My favourite to this day is my Antique Winchester single bolt action .22 rifle. I guess my point is, when Michael pulled up to the SF Gun Exch. I was not worried, but interested in looking. What I was not expecting, that Michael was there to buy bullets. .357 mag, and 44 mag. hollow points. Hollow points are defence rounds. He asked me to use my ID for purchase. (I was not familiar with laws, concerning foreigners and bullets). There were numerous boxes, which he had packed into a strong, leather Harley Bag. We eventually began our drive back to Santa Rosa on Highway 101, when we were pulled over by a California Highway Patrol officer for speeding. (70+ mph).

Michael seemed exciting, and fun. However, I wanted to make sure that this new friendship. would remain just that. So, I had a talk with my father. "Dad, I really like Michael… .as a friend, could you talk to him? Dad agreed.

MONIKA MEETS MICHAEL.

Monika was living in Carmichael, Ca. a suburb of Sacramento, Ca.

She had a good roommate/friend whom she worked with. She enjoyed bowling, and even had her own blue swirled ball, with her name on it, and blue suede shoes. (I have them, to this day) Monika liked to spend time making ceramic items at a shop in the area. She made Halloween, and Christmas figures, and a beautiful gingerbread house cookie jar. These items I have, only because they were gifts, and never went to England.

At some point, Dad asked Monika if she would be interested in letting his new acquaintance visit, take him for a tour of that area, including Tahoe. She agreed, and Michael was on his way.

Things seemed to happen very fast, almost a blur of events over the next few weeks. Monika was on her way to a promising future. True work ethic, a deeply caring nature, friends, admirers, and a loving family. I enjoyed watching her work, during a trip to a car dealership. They needed work done on their computer. I remember the feeling of pride, in being Monika's sister.

This is a moment when writing, that I feel a continued loss. My big sister...how many lessons I could have learned, and guidance that I have not/and will not have. As I write this moment, I am reminded, that today is/would have been Monika's birthday. Happy Birthday Monika... I love you.

Initially, I was excited about Monika, and Michael.

I was young, and happy that this fun, interesting, well spoken English gentleman of about 29, was treating my sister quite well, it seemed. And, as I said to my Dad, I would like to be friends. After all, Michael was already fitting in.

Much of the story, I will try and condense.

Michael did everything that he could, to quickly win over Monika, and our father. Trips, gifts, and promises. Material things were easy for him to produce....the promises? I believe that most, were never meant to be kept. With all that came to Michael from the Vestey Family name and wealth, it was easy for Michael to manipulate, apologise, produce another gift... .and... more promises.

Monika was quickly taken with Michael. I remember how happy she seemed....at first. They came to the family home, I believe it was Thanksgiving. Michael had asked for Monika's hand in marriage, and Dad had gave his blessing.

Then the wedding plans. The wedding would take place in Santa Rosa at Saint Eugene Cathedral. Michael, and Monika began premarital sessions at the church. Monika was enjoying planning her wedding, she showed me the dress that I would wear. All was good, until one of Michael's first lies came out. HE was already married! He kept it from Monika, and lied in a House of God about his ability to be married to Monika.

Finally, the divorce came through, and the wedding was moved to England. Only our parents, and grand-parents were flown to attend. This was the first time, I personally felt off about Michael. Other things that had taken place, seemed to be shadowed by the hole event of Michael's proposal, lie, wedding plans, divorce, and change of venue. I was a bit hurt that my brother, and I were not included. To Monika, it was really more about spending too much. She did seem to be happy, at first. She definitely enjoyed Michael's devoted attention. Michael's connection to Family, and wealth, made it easy for him to swoon Monika.

From that time on, there seemed to be constant drama.

Monika, wished for a loving, trusting, and traditional marriage. Much like that of our parents, and grandparents. She was trying to adapt to a new country, and a very new relationship. She loved to learn, and had applied to Oxford. I seem to remember her using her maiden name. She wanted to try based on her own merit, not because of Michael's Family name. She had passed the entrance exam, but then an unexpected written exam was given to Monika, she was not prepared, and did not pass. She was quite devastated. Yet she continued on, finding other meaningful ways to spend her time.

At some point, Monika tried to get Michael to go to school, or take on some type of job. Somewhere along the line, Dad, (being a business consultant), and Monika, and Michael decided to start a business together creating Redwood Cycle Scene, selling Frank Thomas motorcycle boots. My parents took a second mortgage on their home in Santa Rosa, to have their portion of start up. It started out well, but gradually problems with shipping, quality, and Michael's involvement began to appear.

Monika, was so in love, and dedicated to helping Michael with his physical, and emotional health, and to help him gain independence from his family's financial strings, that she was willing to sometimes, ignore, or excuse many of Michael's ongoing and building temper-tantrums. At the same time, her fear was growing.

I received a call from Monika one day. She was sounding lonely....maybe a bit uncertain. She asked for me to move to England, to Lambourn House. That I could have a horse, and a piano. I have always loved both, and Monika knew this. I did not go. I had responsibility to my first auto loan, a job, and a male friend that I was fond of. I have never lost the thought of "what if". What if I had gone? Would things have ended differently for the good, or bad? Michael could have murdered me too.

Nothing seemed to get better. Michael and all of his lies, control, and manipulation. Who he was, what he did, claims of going to a job that never existed. Fanciful stories, probably of what he wished he could be, but could never be.

He was an immature man, with fits of a spoiled child, and the financial means to do great harm. Michael never knew a true friend... had to buy affection. People were not around Michael because he was a regular bloke... More because of what he had, and what he gave. Much like my first outing to the Chinese restaurant, and movie. It is not that often that you meet someone, and within a very short period of time, is handing you an expensive gift. This giving of extravagant gifts, often to complete strangers, like Rolex watches, was his way of impressing. I guess, some at first would say how generous he was. Just like a drug dealer handing out drugs, only he got people hooked on himself, with money, stories, and gifts. Monika was not happy with this side of Michael, she felt that he was setting himself up to be used.

Monika did develop a drinking problem. She would sometimes have a glass of wine when visiting (before Michael), but certainly not near the trouble she began having in England. Bob Lindsey's book would have her as a falling down, drunk, drug addict, on a regular basis. No.... but she did start to drink, and possibly take some tranquillisers to the point that, when Michael was arrested on firearms possession charges, and was not allowed to leave the UK. Monika came back to CA. and entered herself into Duffy's recovery residential treatment program.

Things just seemed to continue to deteriorate. Michael would have angrier child-like fits, then come back and ask for Monika's forgiveness, bearing more trinkets, including a diamond necklace from Cartier. Sometimes, shutting off all the services in Lambourn House. Other times physically threatening Monika, and actually assaulting her. He had put a gun to her head at one time.

To this very day. My mother at 91 years, still remembers telling Monika "Please, just come home Monika" But she still felt that she loved Michael, and could help him get the mental help he needed.

Unfortunately, Monika was not able to help

Michael recover from his life as a Vestey. The family was less concerned about Michael, then their name. He was their proverbial Black Sheep, and the Lord Spam Klan was not fond of negative attention. Often, if Michael wanted more than his monthly trust allowance, he would just ask Mr. Brown. He would usually get his way, just to keep him happy, and from another jealous fit. He was "believe it or not" often jealous of the opulence, of the rest of the Vestey family.

Michael Planned the murder of my sister. And, it was premeditated. It was not "diminished responsibility". He went to Australia, was able to purchase a weapon, bring it back on a flight coming into Heathrow without detection, bring it home to Lambourn House and laid in wait until my sister came in the door. He opened fire.

After hiding her body in a half-built sauna for numerous months, binging women to the home for sex and giving Monika's jewellery way, as her body sat nearby. Finally, dumping her in Exeter on the side of the road in a pull off. He decapitated her, and hid her head in the boot of a Mini Cooper. "HE" said, because he couldn't do anything to her head, because he loved Monika. ABSOLUTE BULL SHIT! I was more of his sick, twisted plan of cover up. Monika had dental work done in London. Her teeth were now on record in England, with her dentist. To this day, I have a hard time seeing a Mini Cooper, without it becoming an emotional trigger for me.

The "Family" hired the best attorney in the land to get Michael off. They surely knew he was guilty as charged, but having a murderer in the family could not be. My sister was spoke of, and treated like she had caused her own death.

How can you tell when a lawyer is lying? He opens mouth! Same with my former Brother-in-law Sir Lord of Telling Lies.

While preparing for Michael's trial. The family had paid all expenses for his defence, including sending private investigators to Santa Rosa, and Sacramento to get what ever dirt they could on Monika. The paparazzi were hiding around our home, and trying to get my parents to give interviews, etc. offering lots of money. All was turned down. I had moved to Sacramento to get away from the trauma, but it only continued. I was told to take my name off of my mailbox, so it would be harder to be harassed.

Monika's funeral day was so hard. My parents had to negotiate with the Family, in order to have Monika's body returned in a casket. Not cremated. The Vestey's were concerned about a wrongful death lawsuit. They really did not know that there are people in the world, that are not "Sue-Happy". There was no way in hell that my parents would ever what blood money. Just what is right. Often I have had people think that our family somehow profited from Michael's family, or from the book done with Robert Lindsey. No, and No.

Our family has never been the same. Christmas, and other holidays lost their joy and have all been shadowed by the loss of Monika. Never to hear from either her, or Michael again. Monika's belongings, of what the family shipped home, was piled in big boxes. Clothing, smelling of mould, broken unwrapped items, furs and jewellery missing, and adding further insult to Monika, and her family,.apparently the family sold her Pontiac Trans Am Formula 400 to pay towards the storage fees for her belongings. Growing up, Monika dreamed of some day earning a car like that. She had traded in her Fiat Spider towards it, with Michael insisting on sharing the cost.

Monika had a beautiful Cockatoo. She laughingly named "Cocky". She loved the bird, it was a bit of a companion for her. My parents wanted it to come home to the US, but were later told, that it had died during quarantine.

Not a letter of apology for our loss... just Vestey business as usual.

MURDER AND THE AFTERMATH

I sit here at my home office in Oregon USA, haven been given a gift from the gentleman, whose book you are reading.

Steve Thrift has allowed me to write about Monika, and Michael. To put to paper, and to finally put to the public, what my memories are, and experiences have been.... and, for the first time in 37 years, going through this process, is helping me in breaking down the walls of trauma, and to finally feel true peace, and healing.

From the time Monika was taken from our family at only 26 years old, we have struggled. The sadness, and inability to comprehend what had taken place, was so overwhelming.

People from around the world, were trying to get their bits. Somehow, my parents managed to move forward. I would try so hard at every holiday, birthday, etc. to make them happy...so afraid to lose them too.

Over the first 10 years, my brother began heading down hill. Both of us struggled to move on. We were pretty much ignored. Our parents, were not able to support us due to their own pain. Rarely did anyone ask "how are the twins"? We both had problem relationships, we both tried to self-medicate the pain away. At one time, I drank, and tried other ways to numb my pain. I remember sleeping near a park one night in my 1971 Monte Carlo, with my Doberman pincher "Traveler"...feeling so depressed over Monika, and just wanting somewhere to hide and be safe for a night... a sudden knock on my car window had startled me awake. It was a Santa Rosa Police Officer.

He said that I could not sleep there. When the officer saw my name "Erika Zumsteg" on my license, he knew who I was because of all the news about Monika. He told me his name, said to follow him to an area which was his "beat", and that he would keep an eye for my safety, that night. I started uncontrollably crying, eventually thinking that there MUST be a bright side to everything, and at least for tonight, .someone cared, and watched over me.

I suffered, and had allowed abuse in many forms to enter my life, so many times crying out for Monika to still be there for me. For the trauma to go away.I began having serious anxiety, and panic attacks, yet I continued on with the idea that there IS a bright side....

Mark over this time, became an addict/alcoholic. His pain was so great, that he found it hard to function without help. Alcohol at first, some pot, but after a back injury on the job, he was introduced to pain meds, and eventually he became hooked on opioids.

When Robert Lindey's "Irresistible Impulse" was due to be released in three days, that is when our parents informed us that they had worked on the book with Bob. Mark and I, knew nothing at all about this book! I was in school working on pre-requisites to the RN program, and now... ten years later... the media started up again. I was receiving calls from media sources. It was starting again, but I kept trying to finish my classes. I had to let instructors know what was happening, and would ask to leave classes a few minutes early to avoid any media.

Why my folks did not tell Mark, and I about working on the book? Mom said she wanted to protect us. I think that my father needed to be heard, and to speak up for Monika. He felt guilt for even having met Michael that day in Sausalito. For unknowingly, inviting an unstable stranger into our lives.

Within about a month of the release of Lindey's book, my brother was found dead, by my mother, of an overdose.

Just like the night that Michael murdered Monika, felt a strong sense of fear, and panic. It was about 2am on a Sunday morning. Monday I went to take one of my Finals tests at the college, I felt incredibly nervous, and felt the need to finish the test in a hurry... I just had to get out of there and get home. When I got to my house, I found telephone messages telling me that something had happened... hat my brother had expired! I fell to my knees. Now, Mark was also gone. How could I go on.

Around 4-5 months later, my Dad said that Mom and I, should use his air-miles and visit family in Switzerland. I had developed pretty severe PTSD anxiety after losing Mark, and had to be on medication from the doctor to make the trip.... I was worried about my own mortality at this point. Lots of anticipatory anxiety. We stayed about a month. Some years later, my Dad said that he had intended on committing suicide when we were gone. He had taken his hand gun to a beautiful overlook of the Calistoga valley, but was stopped when a couple of motorcycle/Program friends on a ride, noticed him. They saved my Dad's life that day. He pasted away in 2006.

My mother to this day, has never stopped grieving. At 91, she still repeats I told Monika, "just come home" and has a hard time with good memories. She lives with my husband Tom, and I. I continue to do all that I can to make her days as good as possible. Almost every day I live with repeated stories of what a good guy Mark was, and how smart, and caring Monika was. She sometimes says "there is a reason that I had twins" I am so lucky to have you Riki.

I have suffered what one of Monika's English friends called the "The Vestey Curse". As for Michael....he did 10 years, was released back to his life of luxury.....even aloud to leave England and live out his days, in Perth Australia. I learned years back of Michael's death when I was contacted by Paul Murry of the West Australian. He remembered my first words..."I guess that I will never get the change now, will I? He asked what I meant. I said, I will never get the chance to ask Michael....why? I was informed that Michael, due to his diabetes, lost both legs.... Karma?

Sincere thanks, to Steve Thrift. An amazing author, and good investigator....so glad you found me.

APPENDIX
THE MURDER WEAPON

This rifle was purchased by Telling in Australia

Illegally smuggled and possessed by Michael Telling in the UK

It was used by him to murder her, shooting her four times

Winchester Marlin 336W underleaver rifle .30-30

30-30 hollow point, dum - dum ammunition

Weapons taken from Telling on his arrest 23rd January 1982

Colt Python .357 Magnum, Serial Number V28233/H7656937

His similar to the gun taken from him in January 1982, and despite the court case, he purchased this replacement from the Perkins family on December 23rd 1982

Colt AR-15 Civilian

Bullets in the chamber of the guns when Telling was arrested 23rd January 1982

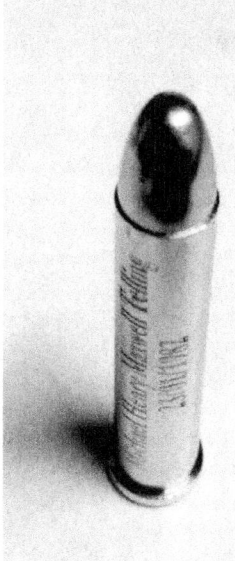

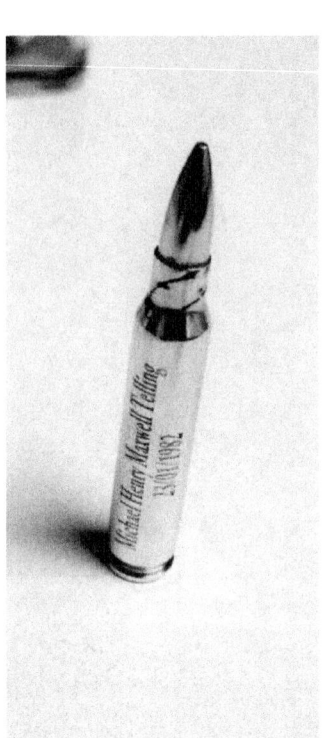

AFTERWORD

A percentage of proceeds from any sales of this book will be donated to: Wycombe Women's Aid, formally known as 'The Home for Battered Women', a short distance from Lambourne House.

And at the request of Riki Bedford, formally Riki Zumsteg, to *ridemyroad.org*, a nonprofit organisation that supports women survivors of sex trafficking in the United States of America.

ACKNOWLEDGMENTS

There are many people that I would like to thank for their assistance in writing this book.

However, and unfortunately, as many attempts have been made to block me from writing this story, even before I started, I would like to name those who have been obstructive in my attempts, and the very, very few that have assisted and / or co-operated. One has to wonder exactly what there is to hide, even after all these years have passed.

I have attempted to contact the following: -

Lord Vestey. Letters, emails unanswered, unacknowledged.

Thames Valley Police. No longer have the evidence or records. In any case, information too sensitive still.

Devon and Cornwall Police. No longer have the evidence or records. In any case, information too sensitive still.

Thames Valley Police Crime Commissioner. Refer you query to Devon and Cornwall.

Devon and Cornwall Crime Commissioner. Refer your query to Thames Valley Police.

UK Home Office. No reply.

Her Majesty's Prison Service. No reply

Australian Federal Police. Require Lord Vestey's consent!

Western Australian Police. No reply.

North Bridge House school. No reply

Pinehurst school. No reply

Maudsley Hospital. Unable to give any information, data protection quoted.

Bredinghurst School board of governors. No reply.

Oliver Westmancott, St. Andrews hospital. *Information refused.*

Hon. George Brandis. The High Commissioner of Australia to the United Kingdom. No reply.

Rt. Hon. Priti Patel, Home Secretary, UK. No reply.

Rt. Hon. Rob Butler MP. Unable and also unwilling to help.

Glenys Joplin, Murdoch Hospice. Too long ago. All records destroyed. 2nd request – no reply

Harley Davidson San Francisco – no reply

Jochen Zeitz, CEO Harley Davidson USA – no reply

Susan Bright – no reply

Thomas Schwartz, Reynolds and Reynolds – no reply

Wilf Chambers, British Car Sales, Perth – no reply x 2

Rt. Hon Elliot Banks, MP. 'I have no relevant information and cannot be of assistance'.

Alison Telling – no reply

Current owners of Lambourne House, now 'Lamburn' – no reply

Linda Blackstock– unable to trace

Susan Bright – unable to trace

Julie Chamberlain – unable to trace

And thanks to the few: -

Michael Dewey – Bucks Free Press, for his research.

Richard Feakin, William Penn school for his memories.

David Stewart, Oceanair International for the calls.

Christina Finlayson and Riki Bedford for the memories and contributions.

And to those who read this, thank you.

I am sure that there are others that I have forgotten, and I apologise for omitting them. Save those named, you have all been of no use whatsoever.

I would, however finally, like to thank Jaynie for her support as always, and this book is also for her.

ABOUT THE AUTHOR

Steve Thrift is the author of 7 true crime novels.

A former investigator, intelligence analyst and close protection specialist, Steve has gained extensive experience over the past 30 years as a working detective, both in and out of the police force.

ALSO BY STEVE THRIFT

Nothing Like the Truth

Jack

Printed in Great Britain
by Amazon